BRF Book Club

Singing to the Lord

Michael Ball

Singing to the Lord

The Psalms as Hymns

Michael Ball MA, DPhil

Minister of Pontypridd United Church

The Bible Reading Fellowship

First Published 1979

BRF Book Club no. 2

The Bible Reading Fellowship

BRF encourages regular informed Bible-reading as a means of renewal in the churches.

BRF publishes daily readings with explanatory notes:

Series A Guidance for the daily reader

Series B Briefer notes with Bible passages printed

Compass Illustrated notes for the 10–13 age-group

Discovery Weekly themes for discoverers of all ages

BRF also publishes introductory booklets on Bible-reading, group study guides, children's aids, audio-visual material, etc.

BRF St Michael's House, 2 Elizabeth Street, London SW1W 9RQ

BRF PO Box M, Winter Park, Florida 32790, USA

BRF Jamieson House, Constitution Avenue, Reid ACT 2601, Australia

Ball, Michael, b.1938

Singing to the Lord.

1. Hymns – History and criticism 2. Bible. Old Testament. Psalms

I. Title II. Bible Reading Fellowship

264'.2 BV310

ISBN 0-900164-44-1

design/print Eyre & Spottiswoode Ltd

General Introduction

'My son, there is something else to watch out for. There is no end to the writing of books, and too much study will wear you out' (Ecclesiastes 12:12). No doubt, the preacher was speculating upon the barrenness of a great deal of his thinking and, as he indicates in the next verse, felt that, if only God was given his rightful place in life, all would fall into place. On the face of it, however, he seems to be suggesting a moratorium on publication! When one considers that volumes upon volumes have been written on the Bible, the question may well arise why the Bible Reading Fellowship should contemplate starting a Book Club, in which the books would actually deal with the Bible. The only justification can be the deep-seated conviction that there is still more to be found in the pages of Scripture – that it is no mere collection of sagas or historical documents, no mere survival from the religious aspirations of near-eastern peoples of a past age. If it were, the Bible would belong to a limited number of scholars interested in ancient literature or antiquities. As it is, this Book Club has been launched in the conviction that the Bible is no dead book, that its message is alive and communicates with contemporary man and contemporary society.

What is more, we can discover the Bible speaking a word of God to us, witnessing to that element of mystery in life, which enables us to break out of the prison of our own thinking and frantic attempts to save ourselves and our world. It speaks of life with a vision, life in response to a calling. It speaks of a God who makes his demands upon us and yet succours us and gives us direction for life. A word from God for us? More, still! For Christians this word finds its focus in the living word, Jesus Christ. For he is discovered as the way to life itself, for he encounters us as 'the way, the truth and the life' (John 14:6).

In his epilogue to the third and final volume of the Cambridge History of the Bible the late Professor Greenslade closed his remarks with reference to 'the Gospel which the Bible perpetually proclaims'. He sees here the reason why, at the coronation of the British monarch, the Bible, when presented to the newly-crowned ruler, can be described as 'the most valuable thing that this world affords'. It was for this reason that Samuel Taylor Coleridge was able to exclaim, 'I do not find the Bible, the Bible finds me'.

Accordingly, the series of books in this new Book Club will indicate that the Bible is much more than a mine from which we may dig up an occasional ingot. The 'gospel' or 'good news' it proclaims impinges on every department of thought and action. The Bible can be misused as well as used. It can become a fetish and be detached from the actualities of human life. If, however, we consider the ways in which the Bible has been, is and can be used, we cannot fail to catch something of its continuing appeal and continuing relevance for today's world.

In *Singing to the Lord* Dr Ball is concerned to say how the Psalms, which were part and parcel of the worship of the Hebrew and then the Jewish church, came into Christian worship. He expands upon the fact that whilst there is a sense in which we reproduce the traditions of the past and so maintain a line of continuous praise and worship, we also adapt the past in the light of our present understanding. This, he feels, is particularly true of the way in which the Psalms have been used. In the movement from Psalms to hymns he sees the desire to express a Christianised version of the Old Testament material which reflects also the experience and the thought-forms of the hymn-writers. From many Churches he illustrates how in the hymn one has a specific and definite Christian re-writing, but nonetheless the Psalms have been the basis for these new developments in Christian prayer and praise. As the chapter titles indicate, Dr Ball sees a continuous tradition of praise from ancient times to our own age. For him the key figure who weds the old and the new is the great hymn-writer Isaac Watts, who was concerned to bring 'new honours for His name'. From the readiness of people in the eighteenth century to express their worship in contemporary idiom Dr Ball brings us at the end of the book to the present day with the demand that our worship, whilst being historic, should still be contemporary, reflecting our modern society and our world-view. Throughout, the author presents clear evidence of the extent to which contemporary hymnodies have drawn upon the language and devotion of the psalter.

R. J. HAMMER

Michael Ball

Born at Woodville (South Derbyshire) in 1938, Michael Ball was educated at Ashby-de-la-Zouch Boys' Grammar School. He studied chemistry at Brasenose College, Oxford and then moved to the Clarendon Laboratory for research and his doctorate.

He trained for the Baptist ministry at Regent's Park College, Oxford and became minister of Turret Green Baptist Church, Ipswich (1965–70). In 1970 he took up his present appointment as minister of Pontypridd United Church. Baptist and United Reformed Church members form a united congregation.

Married, with three children, Dr Ball has been much involved with the Scout Movement. With music as his first 'interest' he has contributed various articles about hymns in the *Baptist Times*.

Contents

Preface

Dr Benjamin Jowett (1817–93), great Oxford scholar and Master of Balliol College, once asked a number of his fellow-dons to name the 'best' Christian hymn. The response he obtained was unanimous – 'O God, our help in ages past'. A century later, the *Penguin Dictionary of Quotations* (published 1960) gives five whole verses of the same hymn, written by Isaac Watts (1674–1748), a distinction accorded to no other hymn or hymn-writer. In every other case, a line or verse is the most that is quoted. Jowett's dons may have been influenced in their choice by the great tune, 'St Anne', to which these words are always sung. Its simplicity, dignity and grandeur ideally match and underline the words and make a substantial contribution to the total hymn. But in the case of 'O God, our help', the words themselves are of such literary distinction that they fully deserve their familiarity and the admiration they have received.

Most Christians in the English-speaking world know this hymn. It appears in every major hymn-book, and many other people probably have memories of it, from school days or Remembrance Day ceremonies. Few would know it in its original form:

Our God, our help in ages past,
  Our hope for years to come,
Our shelter from the stormy blast,
  And our eternal home.

Under the shadow of thy throne
  Thy saints have dwelt secure;
Sufficient is thine arm alone,
  And our defence is sure.

Before the hills in order stood,
  Or earth received her frame,
From everlasting thou art God,
  To endless years the same.

Thy Word commands our flesh to dust,
  'Return ye sons of men';
All nations, rose from earth at first,
  And turn to earth again.

A thousand ages in thy sight
  Are like an evening gone;
Short as the watch that ends the night
  Before the rising sun.

The busy tribes of flesh and blood
  With all their lives and cares,
Are carried downwards by the flood,
  And lost in following years.

Time like an ever-rolling stream
  Bears all its sons away;
They fly forgotten as a dream
  Dies at the opening day.

Like flowery fields the nations stand
  Pleased with the morning-light;
The flowers beneath the Mower's hand
  Lie withering e'er 'tis night.

Our God, our help in ages past,
  Our hope for years to come,
Be thou our guard while troubles last,
  And our eternal home.

In all current hymn-books, it is given in a shortened version and in many, its first line is printed in a much weaker emendation by John Wesley (1703–91): 'O God, our help in ages past'.

The measured and dignified language and rhythms of this hymn admirably match the meaning of the words, and combine to convey accurately Watts' own title for the hymn –

'Man frail and God eternal' – and make it one of the greatest, as well as best-known, of all English hymns. But how many of those who know it and sing it realise that it is a remarkably faithful paraphrase of Psalm 90:1–6 in the King James translation?

> Lord, thou hast been our dwelling place in all generations.
> Before the mountains were brought forth, or ever thou hadst formed the earth and the world, even from everlasting to everlasting, thou art God.
> Thou turnest man to destruction; and sayest, Return, ye children of men.
> For a thousand years in thy sight are but as yesterday when it is past, and as a watch in the night.
> Thou carriest them away as with a flood; they are as a sleep: in the morning they are like grass which groweth up.
> In the morning it flourisheth, and groweth up; in the evening it is cut down, and withereth.

In this book, I hope to tell some of the story of the Psalms and how they have come into Christian worship as hymns, hoping that greater understanding will bring deeper appreciation of the hymns and the Psalms which gave birth to them, and that, for my readers, worship will thus be enriched. The story will be closely linked with the work of Isaac Watts, and may thus seem to be unfair to other hymn-writers, perhaps especially the other great figure in hymnody, Charles Wesley (1707–88). One of the great strengths of the Methodist revival was the way in which Bible, theology and Christian experience were communicated and popularised through song and hymn. For instance, Charles Wesley's hymn 'O Thou who camest from above' is said to incorporate no less than 23 scriptural references and allusions within a very few lines. There is much accuracy in a recent cartoon which depicts a monk studying a book entitled *Teach Yourself Methodism*, singing at the top of his voice! Although Wesley had a similar motive to Watts, to bring the Bible into worship through hymns, his work is not closely linked to the Psalms, and Watts is also the pioneer, and therefore must receive the greater prominence.

Other Christians from very different backgrounds and churchmanship have also endeavoured to make the Psalms a vital part of contemporary worship. Notable among them is Father Joseph Gelineau (1920–), a French Roman Catholic, who has introduced a way of chanting psalms in rather plain new translations to simple musical phrases, using natural speech-rhythms as far as possible. His work has been adapted into English. Others have produced new translations of the Psalms, some specifically designed for chanting or antiphonal reading. Though these developments are of great value, they are not within the scope of this book, and cannot receive more than passing mention.

Unless they are of very specific interest, all the hymns and metrical psalms discussed appear in one or more of the major current British hymn-books or supplements. Where possible, detailed consideration is given to those which are common to most books.

I gladly acknowledge the help I have received from J. C. Henson, J. Harris Hughes and Eric P. Sharpe, and I am grateful to the authors who have allowed me to quote their works – Timothy Dudley-Smith, Brian Foley, Michael Hodgetts, Christopher Idle and Fred Kaan.

I dedicate this book to two families: my natural family with gratitude for their love, patience and encouragement, and the whole family of God's people for nurturing me in Bible-study and worship.

Acknowledgements
Publisher and author acknowledge with thanks permission to use copyright material, given by: Faber Music (for items from the *New Catholic Hymnal*); Falcon Books (for items from *Psalm Praise*); Stainer and Bell (for compositions by Fred Kaan); the Ven. T. Dudley-Smith.

1: From Age to Age

One generation shall praise thy works to another, and shall declare thy mighty acts. *(Psalm 145:4)*

The procession slowly winds its way up the hill of Mount Zion towards the gates of the Temple built by King Solomon. In front walk the Priests, their linen robes beautifully embroidered with purple, red, blue and gold thread. They carry on their shoulders the Ark of God, the visible symbol to them of God's presence with his people. Behind come the Levites with their trumpets, cymbals, harps and other musical instruments, and the great crowd of pilgrims singing, dancing and shouting. They are in jubilant mood, having come to Jerusalem for the annual autumn festival, at once great holy day and holiday. Once again, they have been celebrating the triumph of God over the forces of chaos and darkness which was the creation of the world, and his repeated triumphs in the military victories of his people over their enemies, occasions like the defeat of Jericho under Joshua from their sacred histories.

As the great procession approaches the Temple gates, its leaders engage in dialogue with the senior priests who mount guard there. 'Who is allowed to enter this sanctuary?' they demand. The guardians of the doors reply that those who are pure in thought and deed, who do not tell lies or commit idolatry may enter and find God's blessing. The leaders of the procession claim that they are people who can meet such conditions, and the whole crowd raises the cry – 'Fling wide the gates, open the ancient doors and let the great king come in!' The doorkeepers ask for the correct theological password – 'Who is this great king?' The Temple must not be desecrated by allowing any false or alien god to enter. The procession replies with a confession of faith that the great king is Yahweh, the God who revealed himself to the Jewish people on Mount Sinai, he is Creator, King and Lord. The gatekeepers are either not totally satisfied by this answer, or they repeat their question for solemn emphasis, and again the crowd demands entry for the great king, replying that he is 'Yahweh Sabaoth, the triumphant Lord'. The great doors open, allowing them to stream in and return the Ark to its place in the Temple, before the happy crowd disperses for feasting and celebration, well satisfied that right is right and God is truly victorious.

We have here attempted a reconstruction of the way in which the Jewish people worshipped God in the first Temple in Jerusalem. It is partly based on accounts of worship such as the description in 2 Samuel 6:12–19 of how King David first brought the Ark to Jerusalem to establish the worship of God there. It comes partly from the study of other Middle Eastern religions contemporary with the Old Testament. It also attempts to make meaningful sense of the internal structure of invitations to worship and to enter the Temple, and the questions and answers found in Psalm 24 and others like it:

> The earth is the LORD's[1] and the fulness thereof;
> the world, and they that dwell therein:
> For he hath founded it upon the seas, and established it upon the floods.
> Who shall ascend into the hill of the LORD? or who shall stand in his holy place?
> He that hath clean hands, and a pure heart; who hath not lifted up his soul unto vanity, nor sworn deceitfully.
> He shall receive the blessing from the LORD, and righteousness from the God of his salvation.
> This is the generation of them that seek him, that seek thy face, O Jacob. Selah.[2]
> Lift up your heads, O ye gates; and be ye lift up, ye everlasting doors; and the King of glory shall come in.
> Who is this King of glory? The LORD strong and mighty, the LORD mighty in battle.
> Lift up your heads, O ye gates; even lift them up, ye everlasting doors; and the King of glory shall come in.
> Who is this King of glory? The LORD of hosts, he is the King of glory. Selah.

When Handel set the latter part of this Psalm to music as part of his oratorio *Messiah*, he followed the question and answer format of the words, and allocated them antiphonally to different groups of voices. The first time, the tenors and basses pose the question 'Who is this King of glory?' while the altos and trebles reply. The second time, the roles are reversed. However, it seems unlikely that the original distribution of the words was based on purely aesthetic considerations, and scholars deduce a reconstruction such as that indicated above.[3]

Handel, following the tradition of the Christian Church, uses the Psalm to celebrate the resurrection, ascension and glorification of Jesus Christ, underlining the versatility of the Psalms and their ability to represent the prayers and praises of widely divergent ages and peoples. The description in Psalm 24 of God's triumphal entry in glory takes on a new and deeper significance when used by Christians during the seasons of Advent and Ascension. No longer is the reference simply to the return of the Ark to the Temple, but to God's entry into human affairs and history in the Incarnation of Jesus Christ, or to his victorious return to the true Holy of Holies, the Heavenly Temple, following his conquest over death and hell.

This Psalm has also made a major contribution to Christian worship and devotion through hymns. It appears directly in the versified form known as a 'metrical psalm' by Francis Rous (1579–1659) and William Barton (1597–1678):

> Ye gates, lift up your heads on high;
> ye doors that last for aye,
> Be lifted up, that so the King
> of glory enter may!
> But who of glory is the King?
> The mighty Lord is this,
> Ev'n that same Lord, that great in might
> and strong in battle is.

Ye gates, lift up your heads; ye doors,
  doors that do last for aye,
Be lifted up, that so the King
  of glory enter may!
But who is he that is the King
  of glory? who is this?
The Lord of hosts, and none but he,
  the King of glory is.

The metrical psalms are particularly loved in Scotland, where this is one of the greatest favourites. In some Churches, it has traditionally been sung while the minister and elders in solemn procession bring the bread and wine into the sanctuary for the celebration of the Lord's Supper. Thus, intriguingly, the same words accompany a latter-day procession of God's people bearing the visible symbols of his presence into a building dedicated to his worship!

In some of the verses of a beautiful Advent hymn written by Georg Weissel (1590–1635), translated by Catherine Winkworth, the 'gates' and 'doors' of the original are spiritualised as the human heart:

Lift up your heads, ye mighty gates;
  Behold the King of glory waits,
The King of kings is drawing near,
  The Saviour of the world is here;
Life and salvation doth He bring,
  Wherefore rejoice and gladly sing.

Fling wide the portals of your heart,
  Make it a temple set apart,
From earthly use, for heaven's employ,
  Adorned with prayer, and love, and joy;
So shall your sovereign enter in,
  And new and nobler life begin.

Redeemer, come! I open wide
  My heart to Thee; here, Lord, abide!
Let me Thine inner presence feel,
  Thy grace and love in me reveal;
Thy Holy Spirit guide me on,
  Until the glorious crown be won.

George Wither (1588–1667) makes the more usual application of the Psalm to the Ascension of Christ in his hymn 'To God, with heart and cheerful voice'. The second stanza begins:

Each door and everlasting gate
  To Him hath lifted been;
And in a glorious wise thereat
  Our King is entered in.

Other hymn writers who have used Psalm 24 in their ascension hymns include Mrs C. F. Alexander (1818–95), 'The golden gates are lifted up'; Miss F. R. Havergal (1836–79), 'Golden harps are sounding' and Bishop Christopher Wordsworth (1807–85), 'See the Conqueror mounts in triumph'.

Charles Wesley pursues a more independent line, though one which is thoroughly scriptural, in using the Psalm in one of his hymns in praise of the resurrection:

Our Lord is risen from the dead;
  Our Jesus is gone up on high;
The powers of hell are captive led,
  Dragged to the portals of the sky:
      Alleluia!

Loose all your bars of massy light,
  And wide unfold the ethereal scene;
He claims these mansions as His right;
  Receive the King of Glory in:
      Alleluia!

Who is the King of Glory? who?
  The Lord that all our foes o'ercame,
The world, sin, death, and hell o'erthrew;
  And Jesus is the Conqueror's name:
      Alleluia!

Who is the King of Glory? who?
  The Lord, of boundless power possessed,
The King of saints and angels too;
  God over all, for ever blest:
    Alleluia!

By focussing attention on one particular Psalm, we have begun to indicate how the book of Psalms, originally the hymn-book, or perhaps more accurately, worship-book, of the Jews in Old Testament times, has come to play a part in Christian worship through hymns. This process has often demanded adaptation from their original meaning and application, adaptation begun by the Jews themselves after the fall of Jerusalem, the destruction of King Solomon's Temple and the end of the Davidic dynasty of kings. The degree of adaptation varies. Sometimes we hear an ancient Psalm with modern ears and unconsciously adjust the meaning. Sometimes the very choice of a Psalm for a particular season of the Christian year begins to give it a particular theological emphasis. Sometimes the Psalms receive specific and definite Christian re-writing, to become Christian hymns. Sometimes their influence is more general, by setting a pattern for prayer and praise, or by providing phrases and images borrowed by subsequent writers or used as text for a whole poem. In the rest of the book, we shall investigate the relationship between the Psalms and Christian hymns in greater depth and detail.

[1]'LORD' translates God's name of Yahweh or Jehovah; 'Lord' translates the word meaning 'ruler' or 'king'.

[2]It is not now possible to translate 'Selah'. *See page 11.*

[3]When the Psalms are read in worship, it is usually in unison, or antiphonally. The parallelism of Hebrew poetry, in which meaning is repeated, rather than sound, encourages their suitability for antiphonal reading. I have made some experiments in arranging the Psalms for different groups of voices to read in worship, and some examples will be found in Appendix 1.

2: Worship the Lord

In all his activities he (David) gave thanks to the Holy One, the Most High, in words of glory; he put all his heart into his songs out of love for his Maker.

He placed harps before the altar to make the singing sweeter with their music; he gave the feasts their splendour, the festivals their solemn pomp, causing the Lord's holy name to be praised and the sanctuary to resound from dawn.

Ecclesiasticus 47:8ff. (Jerusalem Bible)

The potential value of a good hymn-book in Christian worship is not always realised. Congregations, church musicians and ministers and clergy are frequently very conservative in their use of hymns, maintaining a very limited repertoire. Congregations are often not trained to take proper notice of the words they sing, and this is partly because those trusted with the choice of hymns do not discharge the task with due care and thought. A London vicar once added a nonsense verse to 'New every morning is the love' in a duplicated service sheet:

New every morning is the moon
The twilight in the afternoon;
The twinkling star, the rising sun
To greet us when the day is done.

His congregation dutifully sang it without murmur or comment!

In the average 'Free Church' or 'Chapel' service, it is the hymns which give liturgical shape to the worship and provide the main opportunities for active congregational participation, so ill-chosen and inappropriate hymns can destroy any internal logic the worship should have. The more formal approach of a Prayer Book service makes unsuitable hymns less of a disaster, since some relevant congregational response and involvement is guaranteed. However, in all traditions, hymns offer a vital opportunity for God's people to participate in worship, and facilitate many kinds of response to God and his Word. Some hymns are wonderful vehicles for expressing praise, thanksgiving and love. Others celebrate God's redemptive and providential activity in creation, in the life of Jesus, in the history of the Church and in the experience of the individual. Some hymns are songs of pilgrimage and mutual encouragement; others are prayers of intercession or petition; others again are expressions of faith or declarations of Christian resolve. Properly integrated with the other elements of the liturgy, the Scripture, the prayers, the sermon, the sacraments, they make an invaluable contribution to Christian worship, experience and devotion.

A truly catholic hymn-book includes material from a great diversity of sources, ages and cultures. Psalm paraphrases from the sixteenth century rub shoulders with translations from the Latin of hymns by early Church Fathers. Jaunty rhymes by Newton, passionate love poems by Wesley and dignified High Church verse from Newman will be there, together with Lutheran hymns of the Reformation and popular pietistical ballads from the American revival tradition. A recent book will also contain some hymns emanating from the younger churches of the Third World. Altogether, there will be a great diversity of material, of varying literary and spiritual values.

Given such an understanding of the scope and liturgical purpose of a hymn-book, it is not misleading to call the book of Psalms 'the hymn-book of the second Jewish Temple'. It too contains material with many different liturgical purposes from various times. As with most hymn-books, the literary and spiritual quality varies from the sublime to the commonplace. The book as we now know it probably dates from about 200 BC, but at least some of its contents are very much older, dating back to David and Solomon, perhaps even further.

There is nothing unique about the Psalms as a literary, religious form. Hymns and prayers designed to be sung or chanted corporately in worship are the common currency of many religions, including other ancient Middle Eastern faiths. For instance, there is extant a lovely hymn to the sun, composed by Pharaoh Akhenaton (Amenophis IV) in the fourteenth century BC, which begins:

> Beautiful is thy rising upon the horizon of heaven, when the living Disc hangs vibrant.
> Thou it is that shineth upon the Eastern horizon, and every land is filled with thy beauty.
> It is thy beauty, thy greatness, and thy splendour that cause praises to thee from every land when thy rays embrace their lands.
> Thou compellest their love of thee, for though thou art far distant, yet do thy rays illumine the earth.

This Egyptian hymn shares with Psalm 104 the concepts of a Creator God, and the total dependence of all life upon him. Thus, compare:

> If there is a chicken speaking within the egg, thou givest it breath within its shell, so that it lives. Thou makest it to unite all its strength, so that it breaketh the egg, cometh forth from the shell and calleth for its mother . . .
>
> Thou hast created the Earth by thy mere wish when thou wast the only one; all men and animals, all that go upon their feet upon the Earth; all that fly by means of their wings.
>
> *(from Prayer of Akhenaton)*

with:

> The young lions roar after their prey, and seek their meat from God . . .
>
> O Lord, how manifold are thy works! in wisdom hast thou made them all . . . *(Psalm 104:21, 24)*

The book of Psalms is not the sum total of Hebrew psalms. The second chapter of Jonah and third chapter of Habbakuk are instances of other psalms or psalm-like material in the Old Testament. Earlier in their history, the Israelites are said to have sung a psalm of triumph to God after the miraculous destruction of the Egyptian army in the Sea of Reeds (Exodus 15). Psalms also continued to be composed after the completion of the canonical books. For instance, the Song of the

Three from the Apocrypha, an addition to the book of Daniel, is a psalm. There is extant a later Jewish book called 'The Psalms of Solomon' whose contents reflect later religious beliefs and convictions. The third Psalm from this collection reveals a fully developed belief in the resurrection of the dead, not to be found in the canonical Psalms:

> But they that fear the Lord shall rise to life eternal,
> And their life shall be in the light of the Lord and shall come to an end no more.

One of the Dead Sea Scrolls, the library of a first-century Jewish sect discovered as recently as 1947, is a volume of hymns or psalms. For instance, number 12 begins:

> I thank thee, O Lord,
> for thou hast enlightened me through thy truth.
> In thy marvellous mysteries, and in thy loving kindness to a man of vanity, and in the greatness of thy mercy to a perverse heart
> thou hast granted me knowledge.
> Who is like thee among the gods, O Lord,
> and who is according to thy truth?

The tradition continues in the New Testament, in the Magnificat, the Benedictus and the Nunc Dimittis from the early chapters of Luke, while in the book of Revelation, John frequently pens psalms of worship:

> Great and marvellous are thy deeds, O Lord God, sovereign over all; just and true are thy ways, thou king of the ages. Who shall not revere thee, Lord, and do homage to thy name? For thou alone art holy. All nations shall come and worship in thy presence, for thy just dealings stand revealed.
> *(Revelation 15:3–4 – New English Bible)*

At quite an early stage of its life, the Christian Church produced the 'Te Deum', for many years the only non-biblical hymn permitted in Matins or Evensong by the Church of England. There is a rich tradition of hymns in

Greek and Latin which continued to be composed during the first fifteen hundred years of the Church, and coming nearer our own time, George Herbert wrote 'Let all the world in every corner sing'; an anonymous Victorian wrote 'Praise him, praise him, all ye little children' – the list is endless. However much we value the old familiar songs, at times it is right to 'sing unto the Lord a new song' and nothing else will serve! We do the Psalms no justice, whatever our view as to their inspiration, by regarding them as some isolated phenomenon. They are a part of an ongoing stream of praise, prayer and thanksgiving through song in worship, offered by God's people throughout their history.

Within the present book of Psalms, clear evidence of earlier collections remains. Eleven Psalms are headed 'to the sons of Korah' and 12 'of Asaph', titles which seem to refer to hereditary guilds of Temple singers. Other headings and words (e.g. 'Selah') probably relate to the original uses of the Psalms, but cannot now be translated with any confidence. They may be rubrics for liturgical use, instructions concerning the music or manner of performance, directions for congregational movement – to shout assent or prostrate themselves, for instance. No surviving detailed descriptions of Temple worship from the period when the Psalms were written, probably about 1000–586 BC, exist, so no certain account of the way the Psalms were used is possible.

The Temple was an extremely busy place, with a large staff of full-time officers – priests, Levites, singers, musicians, prophets and others. Solomon's prayer at the dedication of the Temple (1 Kings 8) gives us some idea of the services which took place. The king himself takes an active, leading part in the worship on this occasion, and doubtless other royal events such as coronations and weddings took place there with appropriate words and music. There were special convocations for national days of mourning or penitence, or prayers for deliverance from plague or military danger. Individuals would also attend for private services or prayer. Solomon also envisages prayers offered by God's people in exile, and pilgrimages to the Temple by foreigners.

In recent years, scholars have classified the Psalms according to their style, content and probable function, and much of the material could very naturally be used in the contexts suggested by Solomon's prayer.[1]

(1) There is a large group of *'Royal Psalms'* which are closely associated with the monarchy – for enthronement ceremonies, anniversaries, before battles and so on (e.g. Psalms 45, 72). Many scholars think that the Davidic kings played a large part in the Temple worship, and that many of the other Psalms were also used by, or on behalf of, the kings.

(2) There are many *'laments'*, some individual, some corporate in nature. If the individual laments were spoken by the king as representing the whole nation, then they too could be corporate in meaning and intention. The plights described are often expressed in quite general terms – sickness, loneliness, betrayal, attack by enemies, demonic forces or foreign armies – and could apply in many different situations (e.g. Psalms 51, 90).

(3) *'Expressions of confidence'* in God sometimes form the endings of the laments. On other occasions, they exist as separate triumphant Psalms (e.g. Psalms 23, 46).

(4) A similar category consists of *'thanksgiving'* for deliverance from various dangers (e.g. Psalm 67).

(5) There are a number of *'songs of pilgrimage'* for the use of worshippers travelling to the Temple (e.g. Psalms 84, 122).

(6) Many of the Psalms are *'hymns'* and *'invitations to praise and fear God'* in the light of his character and activity (e.g. Psalms 147, 148).

(7) Yet others are *'teaching Psalms'* consisting mainly of moral or historical theological material, resembling the wisdom writings of books like Proverbs, or sermons (Psalms 1, 37).

(8) There are further Psalms which do not fall readily into any of these categories, some seeming to be hybrid forms and others the scripts for acts of worship.

The regular worship of the Temple was based on three annual festivals: a kind of harvest festival in the autumn ('Ingathering'); 'Passover' and unleavened bread in the spring; and a summer festival ('Weeks' or 'Pentecost') (see Exodus 23:14ff. and 34:18ff.). These were concerned with the annual cycles of agriculture and horticulture – the rains in due season, freedom from insect pest and blight, sowing and reaping. They were concerned too with God's creation and preservation of the natural world and they celebrated his mighty acts in the history of his people in song and ritual. The description of the conquest of Jericho in Joshua 6 reads more like a religious festival than an act of war, and may give us a picture of the style of some Temple ceremonies. There were also acts of penitence and atonement which helped to ensure God's continued favour.

It is hardly surprising that we find such a diversity of material in the Psalms, if many of them found some place in all the wealth of religious activity which centred on the Temple! With so many human situations described, so many aspects of God's relationships with the world and his people, and so many religious emotions and aspirations represented, it is hardly surprising that the Psalms have never ceased to nourish worship. The basic and striking images and metaphors of the Psalms – floods and mountains, sun and thirst – appeal also to men of every age and culture. The Jewish people continued to use them, long after their original settings in the Temple had become irrelevant, and use them still. The 'Royal Psalms' fed hopes and expectations never realised in David and his dynasty, and so helped give rise to the hope of Messiah, a hope Christians see fulfilled in Jesus – 'Great David's greater Son'. From its earliest days, the Christian Church has also made use of the Psalms, seeing their meaning deepened, extended and renewed by the life and work of Jesus. The Kingship of God, confidence in him in the face of trouble, the recitation of his mighty deeds, his love and care for his people, hope for the future, are all re-born in the light of the Christian revelation, and praise and thanksgiving aspire to new heights.

Let us sing the King Messiah,
  King of righteousness and peace;
Hail Him, all His happy subjects,
  Never let His praises cease:
    Ever hail him;
  Never let His praises cease.[2]

[1]All the Psalms quoted as examples in the following categories form the basis of hymns, and are discussed elsewhere in this book.

[2]From a paraphrase of Psalm 45 by John Ryland (1753–1825).

3: Sing with Understanding

'If a man sing in an unknown tongue, he might as well be a linnet or a poppinjay.' *(John Calvin)*

We have the Reformation to thank for the recovery of everyday language for the worship of God, worship in which the whole congregation could join. For many centuries previously, hymns and Psalms were sung only in Latin by the clergy and specialist choirs. Both Luther and Calvin encouraged congregational singing in the vernacular, but Calvin held to the narrow view that the inspired words of Holy Scripture alone are suitable for the worship of God, and cannot be bettered. As a result, the 'Geneva Psalter' came into being, a collection of versified psalms (known as 'metrical psalms') set to tunes, some of which are still widely used and loved, well beyond the boundaries of Switzerland. British Puritans came into contact with the Geneva Psalter when they fled to the continent during the persecutions under Mary Tudor. The English church in Geneva used metrical psalms in worship from 1556 onwards, and by the middle years of the sixteenth century, collections of metrical psalms in English were appearing in Britain and being sung in worship. From the beginning, Calvin intended the psalms to be the people's main contribution to worship, especially of adoration, thanksgiving and praise. They were introduced to take the place of the responses familiar in the Roman and Anglican Prayer Book traditions.

One early metrical psalm still in widespread use is William Kethe's version of Psalm 100 (Make a joyful noise unto the Lord):

All people that on earth do dwell,
  Sing to the Lord with cheerful voice;
Him serve with mirth, His praise forth tell;
  Come ye before Him and rejoice.

Know that the Lord is God indeed;
  Without our aid He did us make;
We are His folk[1], He doth us feed;
  And for His sheep He doth us take.

O enter then His gates with praise,
  Approach with joy His courts unto;
Praise, laud and bless His name always
  For it is seemly so to do.

For why, the Lord our God is good,
  His mercy is for ever sure;
His truth at all times firmly stood,
  And shall from age to age endure.

The link with Geneva is maintained by the tune, now known rather confusingly as 'Old Hundredth', but a setting of Psalm 134 in the Geneva Psalter.

A large number of Psalters were produced at about this time, notably by Sternhold (d. 1549) and Hopkins (d. 1570?) and also by Tate (1652–1715) and Brady (1659–1726). The story of the many different versions and their inter-relationships is complicated and cannot concern us here.

Metrical psalm-singing did not meet with universal approbation. Queen Elizabeth I is said to have referred to the tunes rather disparagingly as 'Geneva jigs', and Doctor Burney, the musicologist, said that the verses were 'roared aloud like orgies'. The Earl of Rochester was outraged equally by the quality of the poetry and their manner of performance:

Sternhold and Hopkins had great qualms,
When they translated David's Psalms,
  To make the heart right glad:
But had it been King David's fate
To hear thee sing and them translate,
  By God! 'twould set him mad!

Metrical psalms in the Welsh language were not produced until 1621 when Archdeacon Edmund Prys of Merioneth published his psalter, but the Scots adopted them early and have held to them so tenaciously that they have become part of the Protestant Scot's self-image. The Presbyterian *Church Hymnary,* third edition, still contains a higher proportion of metrical psalms than any other major British hymn-book. It is recorded that a Scottish soldier of the 93rd Regiment, 'Quaker' Wallace, went into action in the relief of Lucknow during the Indian Mutiny with the metrical version of Psalm 116 (I love the Lord, because he hath heard my voice) on his lips. According to an eyewitness, he 'quoted a line at every shot fired from his rifle, and at each thrust given by his bayonet':

> I'll of salvation take the cup,
>   on God's name will I call:
> I'll pay my vows now to the Lord
>   before his people all.

Whatever the rights and wrongs of that particular conflict, it is salutary to compare the behaviour of a Scottish 'Christian' soldier with the words of the Indian mystical poet, Rabindranath Tagore: 'The most fearful of all earthly weapons, at the hands of the slaughterers, are those on which have been engraved His own name'.

The Lutherans, like the Calvinists, were thrilled and inspired by the newly-translated wonders of the Bible, and Luther himself wrote psalm paraphrases for worship. He is said to have taken special pains with his prayer based on Psalm 130 (Out of the depths have I cried unto thee), which in Catherine Winkworth's translation begins:

> Out of the depths I cry to Thee,
>   Lord, hear me, I implore Thee;
> Bend down Thy gracious ear to me,
>   Regard my prayer before Thee;
> If Thou rememberest each misdeed,
> If each should have its rightful meed,
>   Who may abide Thy presence?

The greatest of all Lutheran hymns is Luther's version of Psalm 46 (God is our refuge and strength) which he and Melanchthon used to sing together whenever they began to be depressed. In British hymn-books, it generally appears in the fine translation by Thomas Carlyle (1795–1881), 'A safe stronghold our God is still'. This hymn seems almost to embody the spirit of the Reformation. Luther's own tune 'Ein' feste Burg' is quoted by Mendelssohn in his 'Reformation Symphony', and the words have been sung on many notable occasions. Never perhaps with greater effect than on 1 February, 1942 by a great crowd gathered outside the Cathedral of Trondheim in Norway. The local collaborators with the German occupying forces had decided to hold a service to celebrate the appointment of the notorious Quisling as puppet Prime Minister. In spite of objections by the clergy, the usual service of Holy Communion was cancelled to make way for a semi-Christian ceremony. Although armed police prevented the crowd from entering the sanctuary, they were able to make a profound protest against deep wrong, and also express their confidence in the ultimate victory of right, by singing Luther's version of the ancient Psalmist's words:

> With force of arms we nothing can,
> Full soon were we down-ridden;
> But for us fights the proper Man,
> Whom God Himself hath bidden.
> Ask ye, Who is this same?
> Christ Jesus is His name,
> The Lord Sabaoth's Son;
> He and no other one,
> Shall conquer in the battle.

Unlike Calvin, Luther did not think that worship should be restricted to biblical language. He permitted the continued use of older hymns, in translation, and alongside new paraphrases, he authorised the use of newly-written devotional hymns. This attitude has now prevailed almost universally, but made only slow progress in Britain, where Calvin's view was for long dominant. Not until 1821 did the Church of England permit the use of hymns in its official services, though Anglicans like Wither and Newton were writing hymns, and using them at midweek prayer meetings, long before this time.

Quite a number of the early metrical psalms still merit their presence in hymn-books. The popular, almost ubiquitous, version of Psalm 23 –

> The Lord's my Shepherd, I'll not want;
>   He makes me down to lie
> In pastures green; He leadeth me
>   The quiet waters by.

– sung to 'Crimond' or 'Brother James's Air', hardly needs to be quoted. Tate and Brady's simple, but lovely, version of Psalm 42 (As the hart panteth after the water brooks) is another fine example:

> As pants the hart for cooling streams
>   When heated in the chase,
> So longs my soul, O God, for thee,
>   And thy refreshing grace.
>
> For thee, my God, the living God,
>   My thirsty soul doth pine:
> O when shall I behold thy face,
>   Thou majesty divine?
>
> Why restless, why cast down, my soul?
>   Hope still, and thou shalt sing
> The praise of him who is thy God,
>   Thy health's eternal spring.

This version in its cool elegance is far more evocative of longing for God than the rather lumpy contemporary version by Michael Baughen (1930–   ) which appears in *'Psalm Praise'*:

> As the deer longs for water
>   My soul longs for you, Lord,
> My soul is thirsty for the living God –
>   I long to see his face.

We may not often desire God with the passion implied by these words, but in our better moments we may thirst for him, or perhaps wish that we did! In the words which an old saint prayed: 'My God, I do not love thee. I do not even want to love thee. But I want to want to love thee.'

Another fine metrical psalm is:

> Through all the changing scenes of life,
>   In trouble and in joy,
> The praises of my God shall still
>   My heart and tongue employ.

This makes a great hymn of confident pilgrimage, coming from Psalm 34 (I will bless the Lord at all times).

A true metrical psalm is an attempt to versify one of the translations of the Psalms. In the case of older hymns, the translation used is either the King James or the Prayer Book version. The effort of staying as close as possible to a prose original puts great constraint on an author's freedom of expression, and as a result, literary values and even the natural word-order tend to suffer. The second and fourth verses of Rous (1579–1659) and Barton's (1597–1678) version of Psalm 121 (I will lift up mine eyes unto the hills) are prime examples of convoluted word-order and infelicities of expression:

> Thy foot he'll not let slide, nor will
>   He slumber that thee keeps,
> Behold, he that keeps Israel,
>   He slumbers not, nor sleeps.
>
> The Lord shall keep thy soul; he shall
>   Preserve thee from all ill;
> Henceforth thy going out and in
>   God keep for ever will.

It is no easy matter to produce a good verse psalter, especially if rhymes are attempted. Many gifted writers have tried and failed. John Keble (1792–1866) possessed considerable spiritual insight and literary gifts and some of his hymns are widely sung and greatly loved, as, for instance, 'Sun of my soul' and 'New every morning is the love', but not one of his many psalm paraphrases has found its way into general use. Some quite surprising literary and historical figures have written metrical psalm paraphrases, including Queen Elizabeth I whose version of Psalm 14 (The fool hath said in his heart) begins:

Fooles, that true fayth yet never had,
Sayth in their hartes there is no God!
Fylthy they are in their practyse;
Of them not one is godly wyse.

Some other examples are given in Appendix 2 (page 59).

John Milton was only 15-years-of-age when he wrote his well-known version of Psalm 136 (O give thanks unto the Lord; for he is good):

Let us with a gladsome mind,
Praise the Lord, for he is kind.
  For his mercies aye endure,
  Ever faithful, ever sure.

According to Jeremiah (33:11) the words of this chorus were sung each year when men brought their thankofferings into the Temple, while Ezra 3:10–11 tells us that they were used by the Priests and Levites at the foundation of the second Temple in 537 BC. Later in his life, Milton also wrote the Advent hymn 'The Lord will come and not be slow', based on his own translations from the Hebrew of verses from Psalms 85, 82 and 86.

There is no great difference in principle between the metrical psalm, and the psalm paraphrase, but the greater freedom allowed in a paraphrase often leads to more elegant and generally more satisfactory versions for worship. George Herbert (1593–1633) is responsible for a very sensitive version of Psalm 23:

The God of love my Shepherd is,
  And he that doth me feed;
While he is mine and I am his,
  What can I want or need?

He leads me to the tender grass,
  Where I both feed and rest;
Then to the streams that gently pass:
  In both I have the best.

Or if I stray, he doth convert,
  And bring my mind in frame,
And all this not for my desert,
  But for his holy name.

Yea, in death's shady black abode
  Well may I walk, not fear:
For thou art with me, and thy rod
  To guide, thy staff to bear.

Nay, thou dost make me sit and dine,
  Ev'n in my enemies' sight;
My head with oil, my cup with wine
  Runs over day and night.

Surely thy sweet and wondrous love
  Shall measure all my days;
And, as it never shall remove,
  So neither shall my praise.

Joseph Addison (1672–1719) also wrote a paraphrase of the same Psalm, perhaps more notable for its landscape descriptions than its spiritual insight:

The Lord my pasture shall prepare,
  And feed me with a shepherd's care;
His presence shall my wants supply,
  And guard me with a watchful eye;
My noonday walks he shall attend,
  And all my midnight hours defend.

When in the sultry glebe I faint,
  Or on the thirsty mountain pant,
To fertile vales and dewy meads
  My weary, wandering steps he leads,
Where peaceful rivers, soft and slow,
  Amid the verdant landscape flow.

Anyone who has walked in the grounds of Magdalen College, Oxford along the paths still known as 'Addison's Walk' may feel they recognise some of the source of Addison's inspiration. But his delight in the natural world, and thankfulness to God for it, are so genuine as to be infectious!

In *The Spectator* for 23 August, 1712, Addison noted that as Psalm 19:1–3 'furnishes very noble matter for an ode, the reader may see it wrought into the following one', after which he printed for the first time his free paraphrase, now to be found in most hymn-books:

The spacious firmament on high,
  With all the blue, ethereal sky,
And spangled heavens, a shining frame,
  Their great Original proclaim.
The unwearied sun, from day to day,
  Does his Creator's power display,
And publishes to every land
  The works of an almighty hand.

Soon as the evening shades prevail,
  The moon takes up the wondrous tale,
And nightly to the listening earth
  Repeats the story of her birth;
While all the stars that round her burn,
  And all the planets in their turn,
Confirm the tidings, as they roll,
  And spread the truth from pole to pole.

What though in solemn silence all
  Move round the dark terrestrial ball;
What though no real voice nor sound
  Amid their radiant orbs be found;
In reason's ear they all rejoice,
  And utter forth a glorious voice;
For ever singing as they shine,
  'The hand that made us is divine'.

Addison makes no attempt to conceal his eighteenth-century astronomical knowledge. The earth is a ball, with poles, and the planets roll in their orbits – things unheard of by the original psalmist. The specific addition of the moon in the second verse is a stroke of great genius, adding balance and continuity. It is also a happy inspiration to marry Plato's idea of the planets making music in their spheres in heavenly harmony with the Hebrew idea that the heavens speak God's message. So poised, polished and stately is Addison's expression that the very sound of the words evokes the ordered motion and majesty of the heavents – perhaps even more effectively than the original Psalm.

Other standard hymns which are psalm paraphrases include 'Praise the Lord! ye heavens, adore him' (Psalm 148 – Praise ye the Lord) and a version of Psalm 103:1–6 (Bless the Lord, O my soul) by Joachim Neander (1650–80), translated by Catherine Winkworth:

Praise to the Lord, the Almighty, the King of creation;
O my soul, praise him, for he is thy health and salvation:
All ye who hear,
Brothers and sisters, draw near,
Praise him in glad adoration.

The main stream of English hymn-writing flowed in the direction of the original composition, at least until recent times. Charles Wesley (1707–88) only occasionally wrote psalm paraphrases among his six thousand or more hymns. By the standards of his greatest hymns, they are rather ordinary. For instance, his version of Psalm 121 (I will lift up mine eyes):

To the hills I lift mine eyes,
  The everlasting hills;
Streaming thence in fresh supplies,
  My soul the Spirit feels.
Will he not his help afford?
  Help, while yet I ask, is given:
God comes down: the God and Lord
  That made both earth and heaven.

This does not stand comparison with such wonderful hymns as 'Jesu, lover of my soul' or 'O for a thousand tongues to sing'. Metrical versions and paraphrases based on the older translations have continued to be written, but are frequently no significant improvement on existing ones, and have very often failed to find any general acceptance.

The one notable exception is Henry Francis Lyte (1793–1847). In 1834, he published a fairly complete psalter called *The Spirit of the Psalms,* written in the first instance for the use of the church at Lower Brixham, Devon, where he was Perpetual Curate. Several hymns from this volume have come into general use including 'Pleasant are thy courts above' (Psalm 84 – How amiable are thy tabernacles) and 'God of mercy, God of grace' (Psalm 67 – God be merciful unto us, and bless us). Best of them all is the version of Psalm 103 (Bless the Lord, O my soul):

Praise, my soul, the King of heaven;
  To his feet thy tribute bring;
Ransomed, healed, restored, forgiven,
  Who like thee his praise should sing?
  Praise him! Praise him!
  Praise the everlasting King.

This hymn is notable for its lyrical beauty and depth of religious feeling, and is deservedly popular. A detailed comparison reveals that it is remarkably faithful to the original Psalm; no less than 17 of its 22 verses appear in the hymn. By its economy of expression, the hymn even intensifies the wonder aroused by God's dealings with us, so movingly expressed in the Psalm. Thus, Psalm 103:3–4 reads: 'Who forgiveth all thy iniquities; who healeth all thy diseases; Who redeemeth thy life from destruction; who crowneth thee with loving kindness and tender mercies.' The hymn simply and effectively says, 'Ransomed, healed, restored, forgiven'.

In the past few years, there has been a creative outburst in new translations of the Bible which have appeared in almost bewildering numbers. The contemporary language has influenced the wording of prayers and sermons, and the most archaic contents of Christian worship are now very often the hymns. It is not surprising therefore, that there has also been a revival in new hymn writing, and fresh Psalm-based hymns have begun to appear. A few new paraphrases based on the New English Bible appear in the Presbyterian *Church Hymnary,* third edition, published in 1973, and in the same year, a group of Anglican Evangelicals published a near-full metrical psalter called *Psalm Praise.* Their aim is laudable – to popularise the psalter, and bring it more fully into contemporary worship – but in spite of the use of 'you' and 'your' in reference to God, most of the work is essentially conservative, some is frankly poor in quality, and the book as a whole fails to achieve its purpose. However, there are some very valuable contributions. For instance, it is interesting to find a good version of Psalm 37 (Fret not thyself because of evildoers). This is a 'wisdom' psalm, essentially meant for teaching rather than praise, and as such does not usually find its way into hymns:

When lawless men succeed,
And wrong suppresses right
Remember they will fade away
And wither overnight.
Commit your life to God;
Trust him and he will make
The justice of your righteous cause
Shine clear for his Name's sake.

Be still before the Lord,
Be patient as you wait,
And never fret when wickedness
Appears to make men great.
For jealous discontent
Tends only to destroy,
But those who look to God their Lord
His Kingdom shall enjoy.

The godless borrows much
And then cannot pay back,
The righteous gives and gives again,
Is blessed, and has no lack;
The man whose life is right,
His footstep never slips;
The word of God is in his heart,
God's wisdom on his lips.

I've seen an evil man
Firm as a massive tree,
But when I looked that way again
I looked – and where was he?
My steps are from the Lord,
Who helps my feet to stand;
I stumble but I do not fall
For he supports my hand.

Salvation is from God
In times of blatant wrong,
And those who seek his shelter find
A refuge safe and strong.
So fully trust in him;
Shun evil, follow right;
He gives you all your heart's desire
When he is your delight.

(Christopher Idle, 1938–   )

Much more radical and contemporary in his language and thought-forms is Fred Kaan (1929–   ), as shown by his concise, searching version of Psalm 130 (Out of the depths):

Out of our failure to create
  a world of love and care;
out of the depths of human life
  we cry to God in prayer.

Out of the darkness of our time,
  of days forever gone,
our souls are longing for the light
  like watchmen for the dawn.

Out of the depths we cry to him
  whose will is strong and just;
all human hole-and-corner ways
  are by his light exposed.

Hope in the Lord whose timeless love
  gives laughter where we wept;
the Father, who at every point
  his word has given and kept.

Isaac Watts, who saw no merit in singing about obsolete musical instruments, would surely have welcomed Kaan's version of Psalm 150 (Praise ye the Lord) – 'Praise the Lord with joyful cry', whose second verse reads:

Praise him with the sound that swings
  with percussion, brass and strings.
Let the world at every chance
  praise him with a song and dance.

A number of Roman Catholic authors have also composed paraphrases. James Quinn published fifteen in his *New Hymns for All Seasons* (1969) and the *New Catholic Hymnal* (1971) contains some excellent new material. For instance, Brian Foley (1919–   ) contributes this version of Psalm 8 (O Lord, our Lord, how excellent is thy name):

With wonder, Lord, we see your works,
  We see the beauty you have made,
This earth, the skies, all things that are
  In beauty made.

With wonder, Lord, we see your works,
And childlike in our joy we sing
To praise you, bless you, Maker, Lord
of everything.

The stars that fill the skies above,
The sun and moon which give our light,
Are your designing for our use
And our delight.

We praise your works, yet we ourselves
Are works of wonder made by you.
Not far from you in all we are
And all we do.

All you have made is ours to rule,
The birds and beasts at will to tame,
All things to order for the glory
Of your name.

In the same book, Michael Hodgetts (1936–   ) is responsible for a notable version of Psalm 130 (Out of the depths). There are some very fresh rhymes and two striking metaphors – that from book-keeping, and also the 'lonely sentry':

Out of the depths I cry, O Lord,
Let not my pleading go ignored,
But turn in graciousness and hear
What I now ask in hope and fear.

Lord, if you keep accounts with men,
Who can survive your audit then?
But your compassion, Lord, is great,
And in that confidence I wait.

Lord God, my hope, renowned and true,
Your people put their trust in you.
A lonely sentry by the gate,
Keeps watch till dawn: Lord, I too wait.

For in your tender love you gave
  A generous ransom for your slave,
And you will ransom Israel
  From all the slavery of Hell.

Lord who triumphantly arose,
  Give them a place of cool repose,
And let the radiance of your light
  Now dawn for ever on their sight.

It is too soon to know whether these and other modern attempts will prove widely acceptable to God's people in worship. But let us in any case rejoice that the Psalms, which have inspired hymn and prayer for so many centuries, continue to do so today. And let us also rejoice that contemporary versions are being written, even if they do not meet our taste. It is good to be reminded that the praise and worship of God in today's language and thought-forms is always a realistic possibility. However important and valuable is the heritage of the past, the Church can never be a preservation society for the words and the forms of previous generations. A very popular television programme in recent years has been 'The Good Old Days', in which the Victorian and Edwardian 'Music Hall' is re-created, and the audience enters into the spirit of things by dressing in period costume. Although the programme is good entertainment and good fun, its essential appeal is nostalgic, because Music Hall is dead. If it were still alive, period costume would not be needed, even if the old songs were sometimes performed. God is not dead, nor is the Church. Worship is still alive, and the new material which is appearing is proof of that.

[1]In some books the word 'flock' appears here, owing to a printer's error in the old spelling of folk as 'folck' in an early edition of the hymn.

4: New Honours for His Name

Behold the glories of the Lamb
  Before his Father's throne;
Prepare new honours for his name,
  And songs before unknown.
    (A prophetic verse from the first hymn written by Isaac Watts)

Because Latin remained the language of worship for Roman Catholics, and the Anglican Church did not permit hymns, the foundations of the English hymn tradition were laid in the Free Churches, and the founding father was, without contradiction, Isaac Watts (1674–1748), an Independent or Congregationalist. He held the Psalms in deep affection, and wrote some straightforward paraphrases, as for instance (Psalm 36:5–9):

High in the heavens, eternal God,
  Thy goodness in full glory shines;
Thy truth shall break through every cloud
  That veils and darkens thy designs.

Nevertheless, he considered them as defective for Christian praise for three reasons.

Firstly, they emanate from an alien and simpler culture, so that there are things mentioned in the Psalms which retain only antiquarian interest and relevance, while many aspects of life were unknown when the Psalms were written, yet should find a place in worship. For instance, astronomy was not even in its infancy in the days of the Old Testament, yet there are many mentions of sun, moon and stars. Surely a place must also be found for more recent cosmological discoveries in hymnody. On the other hand, it is irrelevant for a congregation of Englishmen in the late seventeenth (or twentieth!) century to sing 'I will praise thee on a psaltery' (Psalm 71:22) when, as Watts pointed out, 'thousands never saw such an instrument'.

Secondly, the Psalms are the hymn-book of the First Covenant, and so include sentiments and aspirations unworthy of the Christian dispensation. We may sympathise with the bitter feelings of the Jewish poet, perhaps an eyewitness of the terrible sufferings of his people during the fall of Jerusalem and exile, when he wrote: 'O daughter of Babylon, who art to be destroyed; happy shall he be that rewardeth thee as thou hast served us. Happy shall he be, that taketh and dasheth thy little ones against the stones' (Psalm 137:8–9).

We may even believe that to be in enmity with God is ultimately destructive of oneself. But anyone who has come close to the mind of Jesus, and is seriously trying to obey his command that we should love our enemies and pray *for* those who persecute us, can hardly use such words in worship or prayer. It is distressing to see that prayers for revenge appear in some of the contemporary psalm versions in *Psalm Praise*. Thus, part of Psalm 56 (Be merciful unto me, O God) in a paraphrase by Timothy Dudley-Smith (1926-) reads:

Merciful and gracious be,
O most High, remember me.
When my enemies assail
May your grace and power prevail.
Keep me in the day of fear
Firm in faith that God is near.

When they wait to do me wrong,
Plan my hurt the whole day long,
Twist my words and mark my way,
Seek my life – O Lord repay!
Wither them beneath your frown;
In displeasure cast them down.

We may not wish to condemn the original psalmist, who lived before Christ, and it is salutary for us to be reminded of the strength of raw human emotions sometimes finding expression in the Psalms, but it is very difficult to justify the deliberate re-working of such unChristian sentiments for the use of Christian congregations in their worship.

The third defect of the Psalms from the Christian point of

view, is that they do not contain the full revelation of the truth as it is in Christ Jesus, even though some parts are prophetic of him, and others may be interpreted in the light of Christian revelation.

Watts therefore set himself to make avowedly Christian and contemporary versions of the Psalms, or, in his own words, to 'make David speak like an English Christian of the eighteenth century'. He called the resulting collection *The Psalms of David Imitated in the Language of the New Testament, and Apply'd to the Christian State and Worship*. Watts not only had the biblical knowledge, the vision and the courage to perform his task, he also possessed considerable literary gifts. Indeed, Dr Johnson regarded him as a major poet. In his hymns, however, he wrote with the average worshipper in mind, limiting his language and use of metaphor, or as he himself put it, he 'clipt his wings'. Nevertheless, he aimed deliberately to improve the literary standard of hymns, and succeeded magnificently.

A typical illustration of his method is to be found in his paraphrase of Psalm 136 (O give thanks unto the Lord), with its recurrent refrain 'for he is good; for his mercy endureth for ever'.

Give to our God immortal praise,
  Mercy and truth are all his ways:
Wonders of grace to God belong,
  Repeat his mercies in your song.

Give to the Lord of lords renown;
  The King of kings with glory crown:
His mercies ever shall endure,
  When lords and kings are known no more.

He built the earth, he spread the sky,
  And fixed the starry lights on high:
Wonders of grace to God belong,
  Repeat his mercies in your song.

He fills the sun with morning light,
  He bids the moon direct the night:
His mercies ever shall endure,
  When suns and moons shall shine no more.

He sent his Son with power to save
  From guilt and darkness and the grave:
Wonders of grace to God belong,
  Repeat his mercies in your song.

Through this vain world he guides our feet,
  And leads us to his heavenly seat;
His mercies ever shall endure,
  When this vain world shall be no more.

Watts avoids any monotony in repetition of the refrain by dividing it into two parts, and alternating it in an *a-b-a-b* pattern, making minor variations even within this overall plan (contrast John Milton's version, page 21). The Psalm's reference to the Exodus of the Jews from Egypt under the leadership of Moses is replaced by reference to God's greater act of redemption in the incarnation and atonement of Jesus. The pilgrimage theme is retained, but transmuted from the Israelites in the desert to the Christian pilgrimage to heaven. We cannot but agree with Watts that 'David left a rich variety of holy songs, but rich as it is, it is still far short of the glorious things we Christians have to sing before the Lord'.

Seen against the attitudes of his time, Watts was being extremely radical. Many Christians believed that only the words of Scripture were fit for the worship of God. All believed in the inspiration of the Bible, and interpreted that doctrine to mean that its very words were given by God in some kind of inspired dictation, so that any tampering was at best impious, and at worst, blasphemous. It is a tribute to the inherent virtues of Watts' hymns, both spiritual and literary, that they so quickly found such widespread acceptance among his fellow-believers of so many different denominations. They also played a major role in establishing the essential value of hymns as part of worship. Watts blazed a trail to be followed by successive hymn-writers to create the great tradition of English hymnody.

Watts firmly 'Christianises' Psalm 72 (Give the king thy judgments, O God) as 'Jesus shall reign where'er the sun'. Like Joseph Addison, Watts was deeply interested in the findings of optical astronomy, and this same hymn contains one of his frequent references to sun, moon and stars – 'Till moons shall wax and wane no more'. Similarly, Psalm 122 (I was glad when they said unto me, Let us go into the house of the Lord) is given a clear Christian content by Watts:

How pleased and blest was I
  To hear the people cry,
Come, let us seek our God today!
  Yes, with a cheerful zeal
  We haste to Zion's hill,
And there our vows and honours pay.

Zion, thrice happy place,
  Adorned with wondrous grace,
And walls of strength embrace thee round;
  In thee our tribes appear,
  To pray, and praise, and hear
The sacred gospel's joyful sound.

There David's greater Son
  Has fixed his royal throne,
He sits for grace and judgment there;
  He bids the saint be glad,
  He makes the sinner sad,
And humble souls rejoice with fear.

In many ways, Watts differs from the popular image of Dissenters of his time. He betrays a pleasant sense of humour in the gentle dig he makes at the anti-hymn factions of his day in 'Come we that love the Lord':

Let those refuse to sing
That never knew our God;
  But children of the heavenly King
May speak their joys abroad.

Although a life-long bachelor, he had a particular love of children and understanding of their nature and needs. He recognised that play is not time-wasting but a physical, emotional and mental necessity for them, and advocated the invention of games to teach them spelling, languages and logic. He would have rejoiced greatly in 'Scrabble'! He wrote special children's hymns which have only fallen out of use comparatively recently. They tend to be moralistic in tone, but with a light and attractive touch. Two of them are parodied by Lewis Carroll in *Alice in Wonderland.* The earnest exhortation to make good use of time:

How doth the little busy bee
  Improve each shining hour,
And gather honey all the day
  From every opening flower!

How skilfully she builds her cell!
  How neat she spreads the wax;
And labours hard to store it well
  With the sweet food she makes.

is transformed into:

How doth the little crocodile
  Improve his shining tail,
And pour the waters of the Nile
  On every golden scale!

How cheerfully he seems to grin,
  How neatly spread his claws,
And welcome little fishes in
  With gently smiling jaws!

Later, the Gryphon asks Alice to repeat ''Tis the voice of the sluggard' (Watts from Proverbs 6:9–10), but all she can manage is ''Tis the voice of the lobster'. Today's children can still enjoy the nonsense, but miss the gentle mocking of sacred things which pleased the original Alice and other Victorian children.

This concern with children appears in his hymns. For instance, in 'Praise ye the Lord! 'Tis good to raise', Watts' version of Psalm 147 (Praise ye the Lord: for it is good to sing praises unto our God). Verse 11 of the Psalm – 'The Lord taketh pleasure in them that fear him, in those that hope in his mercy' becomes:

But saints are lovely in his sight,
He views his children with delight;
He sees their hope, he knows their fear,
And looks, and loves his image there.

Watts clearly understands how loving parents feel towards their children, and uses his insight to develop and extend the New Testament picture of God as Father, the one who notices the fall of the humblest sparrow and who numbers the very hairs of our heads. He celebrates the privilege of being the children of God, in so tender and intimate a relationship with him that we can address him as 'Abba', (best translated not as 'Father' but as 'Daddy') in a particularly moving addition to his version of Psalm 23 (The Lord is my shepherd). The final verses of Watts' paraphrase (My shepherd will supply my need) read:

The sure provisions of my God
Attend me all my days;
O may thy house be mine abode,
And all my work be praise!

There would I find a settled rest,
While others go and come;
No more a stranger or a guest,
But like a child at home.

With no family of his own, and spending some years as resident tutor to the children in someone else's home, perhaps the human domestic joys he missed made him appreciate the more the great joy of belonging by rights to the family of God.

Sometimes Watts oversteps the boundaries of good taste in

updating the Psalms. He was inclined to substitute 'Britain' for 'Israel' rather too easily, producing lines that smack to us of jingoism. His version of Psalm 100 (Make a joyful noise unto the Lord all ye lands) originally began:

Sing to the Lord with joyful voice;
  Let every land his name adore;
The British Isles shall send the noise
  Across the ocean to the shore.

Nations attend before his throne
  With solemn fear, with sacred joy . . .

We are greatly indebted to John Wesley for abandoning the first stanza and amending the second to its now familiar form:

Before Jehovah's aweful throne,
  Ye nations, bow with sacred joy . . .

Not everyone approved of Watts' efforts. Samuel Wesley (1691–1739), older brother of John and Charles, gave voice to his displeasure in the following poem:

Has David *Christ to come* foreshow'd
  Can Christians then aspire
To mend the harmony that flow'd
  From his prophetic lyre?

How curious are their wits, and vain,
  Their erring zeal how bold,
Who durst with meaner dross profane
  His purity of gold!

His Psalms unchanged the saints employ,
  Unchanged our God applies;
They suit th'apostles in their joy,
  The Saviour when He dies.

Let David's pure unaltered lays
Transmit through ages down
To Thee, O David's Lord, our praise!
To Thee, O David's Son!

Incidentally, Samuel is also criticising his more famous brother Charles, who also wrote Christianised psalms. For instance, he redirects the rather fulsome, flattering ode in honour of the king (Psalm 45 – My heart is inditing a good matter: I speak of the things which I have made touching the king: my tongue is the pen of a ready writer. Thou art fairer than the children of men . . .) towards Christ, making a typically passionate hymn of it:

My heart is full of Christ, and longs
Its glorious matter to declare!
Of him I make my loftier songs,
I cannot from his praise forbear;
My ready tongue makes haste to sing
The glories of my heavenly King.

Fairer than all the earth-born race,
Perfect in comeliness thou art;
Replenished are thy lips with grace,
And full of love thy tender heart:
God ever blest! we bow the knee,
And own all fulness dwells in thee.

Others who have followed Watts' lead include James Montgomery (1771–1854) with a Christian paraphrase of Psalm 72 (Give the king thy judgments, O God) – 'Hail to the Lord's anointed, Great David's greater Son!'

Possibly the best and best-known example by a later author is Sir Henry Baker's (1821–77) version of Psalm 23. The two basic metaphors of this Psalm lend themselves very readily to Christian adaptation. The picture of God as shepherd was developed by Jesus in his claim to be the Good Shepherd (John 10:7–16) and in his parable of the Lost Sheep (Luke 15:1–7). The other image, of God as host at a banquet, was also used by Jesus in describing the Kingdom –'many will come from the east and the west and sit down with Abraham, Isaac and Jacob at the feast in the Kingdom of heaven' (Matthew 8:11 in Good News Bible). The same picture inevitably leads Christians to think of the Lord's Supper. All of these associations are made quite explicit by Sir Henry Baker, who also makes mention of 'living waters' (John 4:10) and of the cross:

The King of love my Shepherd is,
  Whose goodness faileth never;
I nothing lack if I am his
  And he is mine for ever.

Where streams of living water flow
  My ransomed soul he leadeth,
And where the verdant pastures grow
  With food celestial feedeth.

Perverse and foolish oft I strayed,
  But yet in love he sought me,
And on his shoulder gently laid,
  And home, rejoicing, brought me.

In death's dark vale I fear no ill
  With thee, dear Lord, beside me;
Thy rod and staff my comfort still,
  Thy cross before to guide me.

Thou spread'st a table in my sight;
  Thy unction grace bestoweth;
And O what transport of delight
  From thy pure chalice floweth!

And so through all the length of days
  Thy goodness faileth never;
Good Shepherd, may I sing thy praise
  Within thy house for ever.

The third verse of this beautiful hymn is said to have been recited by its author on his death bed.

In spite of such splendid precedents, only one Psalm in the

recent *Psalm Praise* is 'Christianised', and then in a half-apologetic manner. The Psalm in question is Psalm 118 (O give thanks unto the Lord; for he is good) whose verse 22 (The stone which the builders refused is become the head stone of the corner) is frequently cited by New Testament writers as a prophecy of Jesus (see, for instance, 1 Peter 2:4, 7). The authors of *Psalm Praise* thus feel there is sufficient justification for writing this interpretation into their paraphrase:

> Christ is the stone banished by the builders;
> Chief cornerstone he has now become.
> This is the miracle God has done,
> Wonderful, marvellous, in our eyes;
> This is the day which the Lord has made,
> We'll sing Hosanna to celebrate:
> Save us, O Lord, we pray,
> This Resurrection day!
>
> *(Christopher Idle, 1938–   )*

Watts, Wesley, Montgomery and Baker have all demonstrated that it is possible to write magnificent Christian hymns by taking a bold and adventurous line with a Psalm, deliberately introducing Christian doctrine and experience. It is a pity that so few hymn-writers have followed their example.

5: Improvisations on Old Themes

And should the well-meant verse I leave behind
With Jesus' lovers an acceptance find,
'Twill heighten e'en the joys of Heaven to know
That in my verse the saints hymn God below.

Bishop Thomas Ken (1637–1711)

It is not possible to catalogue the total influence of the Psalms on Christian hymns, especially when that influence is not direct. None of the hymns of John Keble (1792–1866) in general use is a psalm paraphrase, nor do the Psalms provide the texts by which his hymns were inspired or suggested. Yet in the 'Dedication' of his volume, *The Christian Year*, in which many of his hymns first appeared, he acknowledges his general indebtedness to the Psalms:

O happiest who before thine altar wait,
  With pure hands ever holding up on high
The guiding Star of all who seek thy gate,
  The undying lamp of heavenly Poesy.

Too weak, too wavering for such holy task
  Is my frail arm, O Lord; but I would fain
Track to its source the brightness, I would bask
  In the clear ray that makes thy pathway plain.

I dare not hope with David's harp to chase
  The evil spirit from the troubled breast;
Enough for me if I can find such grace
  To listen to the strain and be at rest.

There are innumerable instances where a Psalm has made a direct contribution to a hymn, through a turn of phrase, an insight or a metaphor. When W. C. Smith (1824–1908) writes of God's justice in 'Immortal, invisible, God only wise', it now seems inevitable that he should compare it to 'mountains high soaring above', probably taking his simile from Psalm 36:6 – 'Thy righteousness is like the great mountains'. When Canon Lewis Hensley (1824–1905) wanted a phrase to describe the power of God's opposition to evil and its forces, he found one ready-made in Psalm 2:9 – 'Thou shalt break them with a rod of iron':

> Thy Kingdom come, O God,
>   Thy rule, O Christ, begin;
> Break with thine iron rod
>   The tyrannies of sin.

J. S. B. Monsell (1811–75) believed that hymns should be more joyful than was frequently the case, and himself composed a popular hymn full of joy and fervour:

> O worship the Lord in the beauty of holiness!
>   Bow down before him, his glory proclaim;
> Gold of obedience and incense of lowliness
>   Bring and adore him; the Lord is his name.

Although obviously inspired by the gifts and worship of the Magi, as recorded in Matthew 3, the hymn is dominated by a line from Psalm 96:9 – 'O worship the Lord in the beauty of holiness'. This not only provides the first line verbatim, but inspires its distinctive rhyme-scheme and sound. As a child, I was always fascinated by the occurrence within one hymn of so many words ending with 'ness', and the ingenuity of the author in finding them and making their meaning fit! Indeed, I believe this hymn introduced me to that aspect of the enjoyment of poetry which consists in the sheer delight in the sound of words and in handling them to make intellectually and aesthetically pleasing patterns, quite apart from their meaning. Hymns have often been criticised, in some cases rightly, as doggerel. While few can be regarded as great poetry, there are some with considerable literary merit, especially when due allowance is made for the fact that they are a popular art-form.

Charles Wesley (1707–88) took Psalm 51:10 – 'Create in me a clean heart, O God; and renew a right spirit within me' – as the text on which he constructed his great hymn 'O for a heart to praise my God', almost a sermon, certainly a meditation in verse:

O for a heart to praise my God,
  A heart from sin set free;
A heart that always feels thy blood,
  So freely spilt for me.

A heart resigned, submissive, meek,
  My great Redeemer's throne;
Where only Christ is heard to speak,
  Where Jesus reigns alone.

A humble, lowly, contrite heart,
  Believing, true and clean;
Which neither life nor death can part
  From him that dwells within.

A heart in every thought renewed,
  And full of love divine;
Perfect and right, and pure and good,
  A copy, Lord, of thine.

Thy nature, gracious Lord, impart,
  Come quickly from above;
Write thy new name upon my heart,
  Thy new best name of love.

There is little more to say by way of Christian comment on the Psalmist's prayer.

Psalm 119, the long meditation on God's law, the Torah, has provided an image frequently borrowed in hymns about the Bible in verse 105 – 'Thy word is a lamp unto my feet, and a light unto my path'. Thus:

We praise thee for the radiance,
  That from the hallowed page,
A lantern to our footsteps,
  Shines on from age to age.

from Bishop W. W. How (1823–97) in 'O Word of God incarnate' and:

Lord, thy word abideth;
  And our footsteps guideth;
Who its truth believeth
  Light and joy receiveth.

by H. W. Baker (1821–77) and the direct paraphrase 'Lamp of our feet whereby we trace our path when wont to stray' by Bernard Barton (1784–1849).

William Cowper (1731–1800) has found his inspiration for a hymn about the Bible in Psalm 19. The first seven verses of this Psalm celebrate the glory of the sun in the sky, while the final verses are in praise of God's Law and its value in helping God's faithful servant to live a good life. There is an implicit comparison between the sun and God's Law. Both in their different ways bring light and life to the world. Cowper makes the comparison quite explicit in 'The Spirit breathes upon the word and brings the truth to sight':

A glory gilds the sacred page,
  Majestic like the sun:
It gives a light to every age;
  It gives, but borrows none.

The hand that gave it still supplies
  The gracious light and heat;
His truths upon the nations rise;
  They rise, but never set.

Let everlasting thanks be thine
  For such a bright display
As makes a world of darkness shine
  With beams of heavenly day.

The psalmist's declaration of love for the Temple – 'Lord, I have loved the habitation of thy house, and the place where thine honour dwelleth' (Psalm 26:8) not surprisingly inspires a Christian hymn about church buildings, namely 'We love the place, O God, wherein thine honour dwells' (William Bullock, 1797–1874). The psalmist's delight in a day of worship and celebration – 'This is the day which the Lord hath made; we will rejoice and be glad in it' (Psalm 118:24) – is echoed by Bishop Christopher Wordsworth in his hymn about Sunday, for Christians the day of the Resurrection and Descent of the Spirit, 'O day of rest and gladness'.

One of the greatest of all hymns is 'Glorious things of thee are spoken' by John Newton (1725–1807), often printed with one verse missing, but here given in full:

Glorious things of thee are spoken
Zion, city of our God!
He, whose word cannot be broken,
Form'd thee for his own abode:
On the Rock of Ages founded,
What can shake thy sure repose?
With salvation's walls surrounded,
Thou may'st smile at all thy foes.

See! the streams of living waters,
Springing from eternal love,
Well supply thy sons and daughters,
And all fear of want remove:
Who can faint while such a river
Ever flows their thirst t'assuage?
Grace, which like the Lord, the Giver,
Never fails from age to age.

Round each habitation hov'ring,
See the cloud and fire appear!
For a glory and a cov'ring,
Shewing that the Lord is near:
Thus deriving from their banner
Light by night and shade by day;
Safe they feed upon the Manna
Which he gives them when they pray.

Blest inhabitants of Zion,
Wash'd in the Redeemer's blood!
Jesus, whom their souls rely on,
Makes them kings and priests to God;
'Tis his love his people raises
Over self to reign as kings
And as priests, his solemn praises
Each for a thank-offering brings.

Saviour, if of Zion's city
I thro' grace a member am;
Let the world deride or pity,
I will glory in thy name:
Fading is the worldling's pleasure,
All his boasted pomp and show;
Solid joys and lasting treasure,
None but Zion's children know.

Newton himself quotes the main biblical references in this hymn. Its first line comes from Psalm 87:3 – 'Glorious things are spoken of thee, O city of God'. Also included are Psalm 132:13, 'For the Lord hath chosen Zion; he hath desired it for his habitation' and Psalm 46:4, 'There is a river, the streams whereof shall make glad the city of God, the holy place of the tabernacles of the Most High'. Also quoted are Isaiah 33:20ff., 'Look upon Zion, the city of our solemnities: thine eyes shall see Jerusalem a quiet habitation, a tabernacle that shall not be taken down . . . But there the glorious Lord will be unto us a place of broad rivers and streams . . . the people that dwell therein shall be forgiven their iniquity'; Isaiah 26:1b, 'We have a strong city; salvation will God appoint for walls and bulwarks'; Matthew 16:18b, 'Upon this rock I build my church; and the gates of hell shall not prevail against it'; and Revelation 1:6a, 'And hath made us kings and priests unto God and his Father'. There are numerous other scriptural allusions, but although incorporating so many quotations and references, this hymn gives no impression of 'scissors and paste' construction. It reads most smoothly, and Newton can only have composed it by living with the Bible for a long time, immersing himself in its thought and expression to such a degree that he could then use then quite naturally himself. A similar gift is shown by his friend William Cowper in another fine hymn, 'Sometimes a light surprises'. Bible-reading for the Christian should be a long-term, not a short-term undertaking. We must not be impatient for quick results, but allow time for the Bible message to sink in and become a part of us.

Enough examples have now been given to show something of the influence of the Psalms on Christian hymns, direct or more distant. If we sing them with sympathy and understanding, they are more than a vehicle for our worship. They are one of the ways in which the fellowship of the saints can become a reality to us. Whatever our denominational allegiance, we are at one with millions of other English-speaking Christians when we sing 'Our (O) God, our help in ages past', 'The Lord's my Shepherd' or 'Praise to the Holiest in the height'. Through translation, we also unite with Christians of other countries and eras, the Reformation in Germany, the great monastic orders, the Church Fathers in East and West. For instance, in:

All creatures of our God and King,
Lift up your voice and with us sing
  Hallelujah, Hallelujah!
Thou burning sun with golden beam,
Thou silver moon with softer gleam,
  O praise him, O praise him,
Hallelujah, hallelujah, hallelujah!

W. H. Draper (1855–1933) permits us to share the joy in all created things of St Francis of Assisi (1182–1226), who was himself inspired to write his 'Canticle of the Sun' on which the hymn is based, by the Psalms, particularly Psalm 148 – 'Praise ye the Lord'.

In

At (In) the name of Jesus,
  Every knee shall bow,
Every tongue confess him
  King of glory now.
'Tis the Father's pleasure
  We should call him Lord,
Who from the beginning
  Was the mighty Word:

Caroline M. Noel (1817–77) has given us a version for singing of Philippians 2:6–11, thought by many scholars to be an early Christian hymn known to St Paul and the church at Philippi. In the Psalms, used directly or through the medium of hymns, we are united with the Holy Family in the synagogue at Nazareth, with Jesus and his disciples, singing after the Last Supper (Matthew 26:30) and with God's people of the Old Covenant, in their joyful Temple worship or sad Exile in Babylon.

This continuity and communion in Psalm and hymn is beautifully expressed by T. H. Gill (1819–1906) in verses from his hymn 'We come unto our fathers' God'. Gill claimed that in writing it, he was 'inspired by a lively delight in my Puritan and Presbyterian forefathers . . . Descended from a Moravian martyr and an ejected minister, I rejoice not a little in the godly Protestant stock from which I spring'. The hymn also owes something to Psalm 90 (Lord, thou hast been our dwelling place in all generations):

We come unto our fathers' God;
  Their Rock is our salvation;
The eternal arms, their dear abode,
  We make our habitation:
We bring thee, Lord, the praise they brought;
  We seek thee as thy saints have sought
    In every generation . . .

Their joy unto their Lord we bring;
  Their song to us descendeth;
The Spirit who in them did sing
  To us his music lendeth:
His song in them, in us, is one;
  We raise it high, we send it on,
    The song that never endeth.

Ye saints to come, take up the strain,
  The same sweet theme endeavour;
Unbroken be the golden chain,
  Keep on the song for ever;
Safe in the same dear dwelling-place,
  Rich with the same eternal grace,
    Bless the same boundless giver.

6: Worship: Historic and yet Contemporary

O may these heavenly pages be
  My ever dear delight;
And still new beauties may I see
  And still increasing light.

Anne Steele (1717–78)

Christianity is an historical religion. This means that certain events in the past are asserted to be revelatory, and the book, the Bible, which records and bears witness to them must retain a unique value and authority. In particular, the events of Jesus are not simply a revelation of God to be perceived by those with spiritual insight, but also the perfect example of God in action in our world.

Now there is a grave danger in accepting the peculiar and unique authority of events in the past, namely that of 'locking up' God in a previous time, of isolating him emotionally and spiritually in an imagined 'Golden Age' of Bible days. According to Jesus, this was one of the faults of the Pharisees, who made fine tombs for the prophets and decorated the monuments of past saints, yet themselves failed to discern God's activity in their own day, and even found themselves in opposition to it (Matthew 23:29ff.). The followers of Jesus have not been immune to the same fault. It is never enough to put the teaching of Jesus two thousand years ago on a pedestal and revere it. We must try to discover his mind now. It is not sufficient to admire and understand the parables he told. In order to be truly faithful to him, we must learn to view our own experience of the world and events in our time as potential revelations of God's nature and ways. The Holy Spirit has been given to lead God's people into the truth, and those who will only stay on ground hallowed by the experience and authority of the past are lacking in faith, allowing themselves to be governed by fear of the unknown (Hebrews 10:39). God is of course consistent with himself, so that any new revelations and insights must always be referred back to the Bible. But the Bible should be viewed as the starting point, the nucleus upon which growth takes place, not the final boundary within which Christians must remain. In an age such as ours, which is still seeing cultural, social and intellectual changes of unprecedented magnitude, it is of fundamental importance that we move beyond the Bible world if Christian teaching is to be relevant to the real issues and problems of faith today and tomorrow.

Our study of Psalms and hymns has shown how previous generations faced this issue in the particular context of worship. We have also seen how God's blessing has been upon the more adventurous attitude. Many Christians in the sixteenth century and afterwards followed the teaching of Calvin, and regarded the words of the Bible as adequate for worship. Indeed, they went so far as to consider 'man-made' verses or hymns quite inappropriate or improper. Other Christians, whether deliberately or in the light of their own experience, followed Luther. He valued the words of Scripture very highly, but was unwilling to be confined by them. In Britain, Isaac Watts was the foremost proponent of this attitude. He took an amazingly radical line in altering the words of Scripture to introduce Christian teaching to the Psalms, and to bring them up to date.

Not many hymn-writers have been so brave, though there are signs that this is now beginning to change. For instance, early hymn-writers such as Watts and Addison were deeply interested in the results of what was then modern astronomy, and refer to it in their hymns. In 'Jesus shall reign, where'er the sun', Watts has the line 'till *moons* shall wax and wane no more'. The psalmist who wrote Psalm 72, on which it is based, had no inkling that there is more than one moon, since the moons of Jupiter and Saturn need an optical telescope for observation. But the psalmist's ignorance did not deter Watts from introducing modern knowledge to the congregations who sang his hymns! Only recently have science and technology again been allowed to find their way into Christian praise (and poetry generally!). For too long, hymn-writers were conservative in their ways, or even actively hostile to contemporary discoveries. However, it is good to see that Sydney Carter (1915–) brings up-to-date astronomical and cosmological thought into one of his songs. Most scientists now believe that there are countless millions of stars with planets, and that on at least some of them, intelligent life must have evolved, or will one day do so. If God is the loving Father we Christians believe he is, argues Carter in 'Every star shall sing a carol', then he will make himself known to them in some appropriate way, as to us:

> Who can tell what other cradle,
>   High above the Milky Way
> Still may rock the King of Heaven
>   On another Christmas Day?

The psalmists often called upon the whole creation to praise God (e.g. Psalm 148). Our understanding of the vastness of creation is now much greater, and must go beyond the evidence of our eyes alone, and the content of the natural world, to include the discoveries of science and achievements of technology:

> God of concrete, God of steel,
> God of piston and of wheel,
> God of pylon, God of steam,
> God of girder and of beam,
> God of atom, God of mine,
> All the world of power is thine!
>
> *(Richard Jones, 1926–)*

Such contemporary writers are not only being faithful to the precedent of Watts and others, but also to the vision and trust of the original psalmists, who saw the wonder and majesty of God in all things.

However much we value the Psalms, chanted or read, in metrical versions or paraphrases, our worship would be greatly impoverished if we did not also go beyond them. There are few Christians now who would regret that Luther's view has prevailed almost universally against Calvin's. Most would feel the loss severely if we were deprived of such spiritual classics as 'When I survey the wondrous cross', 'How sweet the name of Jesus sounds', 'Love divine, all loves excelling' and many others. The faith of Watts, showing itself in his willingness to move forward into new territory for worship, has been richly rewarded by God in the great tradition of English hymnody which we inherit, a source of untold blessing to God's people. Surely similar faith today will be similarly rewarded.

We have seen how the roots of the English hymn tradition lie in the Reformation and its rediscovery of the vernacular in the life of the Church. It follows that most of our hymns are influenced by the King James version of the Bible, or by the translation of the Psalms in the Book of Common Prayer, both of which reigned unchallenged in the life of the Churches for about three centuries. Recent years have brought dramatic changes with the introduction of modern language services, new psalters, and a wealth of new translations of the Bible. Hymns are rapidly becoming the most archaic part of Christian worship, both in language and thought-forms. In some ways, the Reformation battle for the use of the vernacular is being fought all over again. Religion is always a great bastion of conservatism, and there are many to lament and oppose changes in language and content of worship on the grounds of spirituality, tradition and aesthetics. No doubt the Apostles found it painful to translate the words of Jesus from the Aramaic in which they heard him speak, into the common-language Greek of their times, in which they wrote our Gospels. Sometimes, the original Aramaic phrases survive, particularly in Mark's Gospel (e.g. Mark 5:41). However, the Apostles understood that God's word to mankind is universal and must not be made unnecessarily difficult to comprehend. Faithfulness to their insight and example must always demand the use of the vernacular, not a foreign language nor an esoteric antique or literary 'dialect'.

As the words of the King James and Prayer Book translations become less familiar to new generations of Christians, so the scriptural references and basis of many hymns will become less obvious. Only time will tell whether any of the rival translations at present in general use – the Revised Standard Version, Jerusalem Bible, New English Bible or Good News Bible – will establish itself among the majority of Christians, as did the King James version. But we can be confident that these new translations will bring new life into worship. Already, hymn-writers in the Roman Catholic Church such as Fr Brian Foley and Michael Hodgetts are producing new hymns and paraphrases, based on contemporary translations and understandings. In the Anglican Church, we have *Psalm Praise*, which contains at least one splendid hymn inspired by the New English Bible, a version of the Magnificat by Timothy Dudley-Smith (1926–):

> Tell out, my soul, the greatness of the Lord:
> Unnumbered blessings, give my spirit voice;
> Tender to me the promise of his word;
> In God my Saviour shall my heart rejoice.
>
> Tell out, my soul, the greatness of his name:
> Make known his might, the deeds his arm has done;
> His mercy sure, from age to age the same;
> His holy name, the Lord, the Mighty One.
>
> Tell out, my soul, the greatness of his might:
> Powers and dominions lay their glory by;
> Proud hearts and stubborn wills are put to flight,
> The hungry fed, the humble lifted high.
>
> Tell out, my soul, the glories of his word:
> Firm is his promise, and his mercy sure.
> Tell out, my soul, the greatness of the Lord
> To children's children and for evermore.

Perhaps we may be permitted to count the Magnificat as a New Testament psalm! Writers are also at work in other Churches and denominations, and it seems that we may well be at the beginning of a glorious new chapter of hymnody, inspired afresh by the Bible in our own language. Perhaps God will yet raise a latter-day Isaac Watts, with the literary and spiritual gifts to 'make David speak like an English-speaking Christian of the twentieth century'.

Much of this book has necessarily been concerned with the text of hymns, and it is my hope and prayer that those who have read it will sing with greater attention and understanding as a result, proving their love in worship with minds as well as hearts. But even more, may we be led back to the Psalms themselves, the source and inspiration of so many great hymns. The publication of new metrical psalms and paraphrases proves that they retain all their ancient power to nourish prayer and devotion, to provide words for worship, and to lead us to God himself.

Appendix 1

Some Psalms arranged for Responsive Reading

Psalm 24

All The earth is the Lord's and all that is in it, the world and all its people.
He built it on the deep waters and laid its foundations in the ocean depths.

C (The congregation) Who has the right to climb the Lord's mountain? Who is allowed to stand in his holy temple?

M (The minister) The man whose hands are clean, whose heart is pure, who does not worship idols or make false promises. The Lord will bless him and God his saviour will comfort him.

C Such are the people who come to God, who come into the presence of the God of Jacob.

L (The people on the left of the building) Fling wide the gates! Open the ancient doors! and the great king will come in.

R (The people on the right) Who is this great king?

L He is the Lord, strong and mighty, victorious in battle!

R Fling wide the gates! Open the ancient doors! and the great king will come in.

L Who is this great king?

R He is our God, the Lord of power, he is the great king!

Psalm 46

All God is our refuge and our strength, always ready to help when troubles come.

M Even if the world itself gives way, and the foundations of our lives are shaken –

C We shall not be afraid;

M Even if the familiar landmarks of life disappear –

C The Lord of power is with us;

M Even if confusion threatens and emptiness seems about to swallow us –

C The God of Jacob is our stronghold.

M I saw a stream of living water, bringing joy to the holy city.

C God lives there, so it can never be destroyed. His help comes like the light at dawn.

M Nations may destroy each other, civilisations may perish, even the world may dissolve away –

C But the Lord of power is with us, the God of Jacob is our stronghold.

M Look at the world round about you; read the pages of history; and think about what he has achieved. Relax, and know that he is God, ruler of every nation, ruler of the whole world.

All The Lord of power is with us, the God of Jacob is our stronghold.

Psalm 95

M Come, let us joyfully praise the Lord, let us sing at the top of our voices to God, the rock of our salvation.

C Let us come into his presence giving thanks, singing songs of praise in his honour.

M The Lord is a powerful God, a greater king than all other gods. He rules over all the earth, from the deepest caves to the highest mountains. The sea belongs to him, because he made it; so does the land because he shaped it with his hands.

C Come, let us bow before him in worship, let us kneel before the Lord who made us. He alone is our God, our shepherd, and we are his people, the flock he cares for.

M If only we listen to his voice and obey him, if only we rely on him completely, then we shall know his power today.

Appendix 2

Some Psalm Paraphrases by Literary Figures

1. *Psalm 139* *Sir Philip Sidney (1554–86)* and *Mary, Lady Pembroke (1561–1621)*

O Lord, in me there lieth nought
But to thy search revealèd lies;
For when I sit
Thou markest it,
No less thou notest when I rise;
The closet of my thought
Hath open windows to thine eyes.

Thou walkest with me when I walk;
When to my bed for rest I go,
I find thee there,
And everywhere;
Not youngest thought in me doth grow,
No, not one word I cast to talk,
But yet, unuttered, thou dost know.

Do thou thy best, O secret night,
In sable veil to cover me;
The sable pall
Shall vainly fall,
With day unmasked my night shall be:
For night is day and darkness light,
O Father of all lights, to thee.

2. *Psalm 137* *William Cowper (1731–1800)*

To Babylon's proud waters brought,
 In bondage where we lay,
With tears on Sion's hill we thought,
 And sighed our hours away;
Neglected on the willows hung
Our useless harps, while every tongue
 Bewailed the fatal day.

Then did the base insulting foe
 Some joyous notes demand,
Such as in Sion used to flow
 From Judah's happy band –
Alas! what joyous notes have we,
Our country spoiled, no longer free,
 And in a foreign land?

O Solyma! if e'er thy praise
 Be silent in my song,
Rude and unpleasing be the lays,
 And artless be my tongue!
Thy name my fancy still employs;
To thee, great fountain of my joys
 My sweetest airs belong.

Remember, Lord! that hostile sound,
 When Edom's children cried,
Raz'd be her turrets to the ground,
 And humbled be her pride!
Remember, Lord! and let the foe
The terrors of thy vengeance know –
 The vengeance they defied.

Thou too, great Babylon, shalt fall
 A victim to our God;
Thy monstrous crimes already call
 For heaven's chastising rod.
Happy who shall thy little ones
Relentless dash against the stones
 And spread their limbs abroad.

3. *Psalm 1 Robert Burns (1759–96)*

The man, in life where-ever plac'd
  Hath happiness in store,
Who walks not in the wicked's way
  Nor learns their guilty lore!

Nor from the seat of scornful Pride
  Casts forth his eyes abroad,
But with humility and awe
  Still walks before his God.

That man shall flourish like the trees
  Which by the streamlets grow;
The fruitful top is spread on high
  And firm the root below.

But he whose blossoms bud in guilt
  Shall to the ground be cast
And like the rootless stubble tost,
  Before the sweeping blast.

For why, that God the good adore
  Hath giv'n them peace and rest
But hath decreed that wicked men
  Shall ne'er be truly blest.

4. *Psalm 137 George Gordon, Lord Byron (1788–1824)*

We sat down and wept by the waters
  Of Babel, and thought of the day
When our foe in the hue of his slaughters,
  Made Salem's high places his prey;
And ye, oh her desolate daughters!
  Were scattered all weeping away.

While sadly we gazed on the river
  Which roll'd on in freedom below,
They demanded the song; but, oh never
  That triumph the stranger shall know!
May this right hand be withered for ever,
  Ere it string our high harp for the foe!

On the willows that harp is suspended,
  Oh Salem! its sound should be free;
And the hour when thy glories were ended
  But left me that token of thee;
And ne'er shall its soft tones be blended
  With the voice of the spoiler by me!

List of Psalm-based Hymns (grouped under Psalms)

The hymn-books consulted for this work, and whose hymns are included in this list are:
Baptist Hymn Book (1962)
BBC Hymn Book (1951)
Church Hymnary, Third Edition (1973)
Congregational Praise (1951)
English Hymnal (1906)
Hymns Ancient and Modern Revised (1950)
Methodist Hymn Book (1933)
Songs of Praise (Englarged Edition) (1931)

The following supplements are also included:
Hymns and Songs (Methodist) (1969)
100 Hymns for Today (Hymns Ancient and Modern) (1969)
New Church Praise (URC) (1975)
Praise for Today (Baptist) (1974)

Although in the text we have quoted from *Psalm Praise* (1973) and the *New Catholic Hymnal* (1971), hymns from these sources are not included in this list, unless they appear in another hymn-book. The material in *Psalm Praise* is already classified under the original Psalm numbers, and we have not extended the scope of the present book to include Catholic hymnals in general.

Psalm 8
How excellent in all the earth . . .
With wonder, Lord, we see your works . . .
Psalm 9
God shall endure for aye . . .
Thee will I praise with all my heart . . .
Psalm 14
Praise the Lord who reigns above . . .
Psalm 15
Come, O come, in pious lays . . .*
Within thy tabernacle, Lord . . .
Psalm 16
Keep me, O God of grace . . .
Psalm 18
O God my strength and fortitude . . .
Whom shall we love like thee . . .
Psalm 19
God of the morning . . .*
God's law is perfect, and converts . . .
God's perfect law revives the soul . . .
The heavens declare thy glory, Lord . . .
The spacious firmament on high . . .

*Indicates that the hymn concerned is based on more than one psalm.

Psalm 21
The Queen (King), O God, her (his) heart . . .
Psalm 23
My Shepherd will supply my needs . . .
The God of love my Shepherd is . . .
The King of love my Shepherd is . . .
The Lord my pasture shall prepare . . .
The Lord's my Shepherd . . .
Psalm 24
Golden harps are sounding . . .
Hail the day that sees him rise . . . (some books only)
Lift up your heads, ye mighty gates . . .
Our Lord is risen from the dead . . .
See the Conqueror mounts in triumph . . .
The earth belongs unto the Lord . . .
The golden gates are lifted up . . .
To God with heart and cheerful voice . . .
Ye gates, lift up your heads on high . . .
Psalm 25
Show me thy ways, O Lord . . .
Psalm 26
Mine hands in innocence, O Lord . . .
Psalm 27
God is my strong salvation . . .
The Lord's my light and saving health . . .
Psalm 33
Ye righteous, in the Lord rejoice . . .
Psalm 34
God will I bless all time; his praise . . .
Through all the changing scenes of life . . .
Psalm 36
High in the heavens, eternal God . . .
Thy mercy, Lord, is in the heavens . . .
Psalm 40
Day after day I sought the Lord . . .
I waited for the Lord my God . . .
Psalm 42
As pants the hart . . .
Psalm 43
O send thy light forth and thy truth . . .
Psalm 45
Let us sing the King Messiah . . .
My heart is full of Christ . . .
Psalm 46
A fortress sure is God our King . . .
A safe stronghold our God is still . . .
God is our refuge and our strength . . .
God is the refuge of his saints . . .
Psalm 51
Have mercy, Lord, on me . . .
O God, be gracious to me in thy love . . .

Psalm 93
The Lord doth reign, and clothed is he . . .
The Lord Jehovah reigns . . .
Psalm 95
O come, and let us to the Lord . . .
O come, let us sing to the Lord . . .
Psalm 96
In beauty of his holiness . . .
O sing a new song to the Lord . . .
Psalm 98
New songs of celebration render . . .
Raise the psalm; let earth adoring . . .
Sing a new song to Jehovah . . .
Psalm 100
All people that on earth do dwell . . .
Before Jehovah's aweful throne . . .
(Before the almighty Father's throne . . .)
Serve the Lord with joy and gladness . . .
Psalm 102
Thou shalt arise, and mercy yet . . .
Psalm 103
My soul repeat his praise . . .
O bless the Lord, my soul! . . .
O thou, my soul, bless God the Lord . . .
Praise, my soul, the King of heaven . . .
Praise to the Lord, the Almighty . . .*
Such pity as a father hath . . .
The Lord preparèd hath his throne . . .
Psalm 104
My soul, praise the Lord! . . .
O worship the King . . .
Psalm 106
Give praise and thanks unto the Lord . . .
Psalm 108
My God, my King, thy praise I sing . . .
Psalm 113
Praise the Lord! Praise, you servants of the Lord . . .
Psalm 116
I'll of salvation take the cup . . .
I love the Lord, because my voice . . .
Pray that Jerusalem may have . . .*
What shall I render to my God . . .
Psalm 117
From all that dwell below the skies . . .
Psalm 118
O set ye open unto me . . .
This is the day the Lord hath made . . .

Psalm 119
Enter thy courts thou word of life . . .
Teach me, O Lord, the perfect way . . .
Psalm 121
I to the hills will lift mine eyes . . .
To the hills I lift mine eyes . . .
Up to those bright and gladsome hills . . .
Psalm 122
Glad was my heart to hear . . .
How pleased and blest was I . . .
I joy'd when to the house of God . . .
Pray that Jerusalem may have . . .*
The festal morn, O God, is come . . .
Psalm 124
Now Israel may say, and that truly . . .
Psalm 125
Who in the Lord confide . . .
Psalm 126
When Zion's bondage God turned back . . .
Psalm 130
From the deeps of grief and fear . . .
Lord, from the depths to thee I cried . . .
Out of our failure to create . . .
Out of the deep I call . . .
Out of the depths I cry to thee . . .
Psalm 131
Quiet, Lord, my froward heart . . .
Psalm 133
Pray that Jerusalem may have . . .*
Psalm 136
Give to our God immortal praise . . .
Let us with a gladsome mind . . .
Praise God, for he is kind . . .
Praise, O praise our God and King! . . .
Psalm 139
In all my vast concerns with thee . . .
O Lord, in me there lieth nought . . .
Thou art before me, Lord, thou art behind . . .
Psalm 143
O, hear my prayer, Lord . . .
Psalm 145
Good unto all men is the Lord . . .
Long as I live I'll bless thy name . . .
My God, my King, thy various praise . . .
O Lord, thou art my God and King . . .
Sing to the Lord a joyful song . . .
Sweet is the memory of thy grace . . .
We would extol thee, ever-blessèd Lord . . .
Psalm 146
I'll praise my Maker while I've breath . . .

Psalm 147
Hosanna! Music is divine . . .
Praise ye the Lord; for it is good . . .
Praise ye the Lord! 'Tis good to raise . . .

Psalm 148
All creatures of our God and King . . .
Come, O come in pious lays . . .*
O praise ye the Lord! praise him in the height . . .*
Praise the Lord of heaven; praise him in the height . . .
Praise the Lord! Ye heavens adore him . . .
The Lord of heaven confess . . .
Wide as his vast dominion lies . . .
Ye boundless realms of joy . . .

Psalm 150
Come, O come in pious lays . . .*
O praise ye the Lord! praise him in the height . . .*
Praise the Lord, his glories show . . .
Praise the Lord with joyful cry . . .
Praise to the Lord, the Almighty . . .*
Praise ye the Lord, God's praise within . . .

Biographical Notes on Hymn-Writers

Addison, Joseph (1672–1719) Politician, journalist and literary figure, best known for his association with Sir Richard Steele in the *Tatler*, the *Spectator* and the *Guardian*. Wrote five hymns.

Alexander, Mrs Cecil Frances (1823–95) Wife of (Anglican) Archbishop of Armagh, writer of many hymns and much poetry. Her best hymns were written for children, based on the Church Catechism, for instance 'There is a green hill' and 'Once in royal David's city'.

Baker, Sir Henry Williams (1821–77) Vicar of Monkland, near Leominster. For 20 years, Chairman and driving force of the committee responsible for 'Hymns Ancient and Modern'. Wrote many hymns himself.

Barton, Bernard (1784–1849) Quaker, friend of many literary figures, including Fitzgerald, Lamb and Byron. Wrote eight volumes of poetry.

Barton, William (1597–1678) Puritan, vicar of St Martin's, Leicester. Composed metrical psalms which, together with those of Francis Rous (*q.v.*) formed the basis of the Scottish Psalter. Also wrote hymns which influenced and dissatisfied Isaac Watts (*q.v.*).

Baughen, Michael (1930–) Various Anglican offices. Vicar of All Souls, Langham Place, London. Actively involved in writing and editing popular and youth hymns and tunes.

Brady, Nicholas (1659–1726) Irishman who became a minister in the Church of England. Some other literary work, but best known for collaboration with Nahum Tate (*q.v.*) in *The New Version of the Psalms*, collection of metrical psalms which slowly supplanted that of Sternhold and Hopkins (*q.v.*).

Bullock, William (1794–1874) For 33 years a missionary to, and ultimately, Dean of, Nova Scotia with the Society for the Propagation of the Gospel. 'We love the place, O God' was written for the dedication of a new church at Trinity Bay, Newfoundland.

Carlyle, Thomas (1795–1881) Scottish literary figure, very religious, but subscribing to no official creed.
Carter, Sydney (1915–) English folksong writer and performer. A number of his songs are religious, and some, notably 'Lord of the dance' ('I danced in the morning') have achieved international popularity.
Cowper, William (1731–1800) Distinguished poet, letter-writer and essayist. Subject to severe bouts of depression. Friend of John Newton (*q.v.*) with whom he collaborated in hymn-writing and other evangelistic work in Olney.
Draper, William Henry (1855–1933) Anglican clergyman, held various appointments. Translator and writer of hymns.
Dudley-Smith, Timothy (1926–) Has held various Anglican appointments, presently Archdeacon of Norwich. Contributor to *Psalm Praise*.
Foley, Brian (1919–) Roman Catholic priest, has held various appointments in the North of England. Contributed 14 hymns and paraphrases to the *New Catholic Hymnal*.
Francis, St (of Assisi) (1182–1226) Founder of the Franciscan Order. One of the most attractive Christian figures, notable for his love of nature and mankind. His hymns are among the earliest metrical poems in the Italian language.
Gill, Thomas Hornblower (1819–1906) Born into a Unitarian family, came into orthodox Christianity partly as a result of comparing the 'native force and fullness of Watts' hymns' with their 'shrunken and mutilated' versions in Unitarian books. Became an enthusiastic Evangelical Anglican, devoted to all things Puritan and Protestant. Wrote a number of hymns.
Havergal, Frances Ridley (1836–79) Daughter of the Rev. W. H. Havergal, also a hymn-writer of some distinction. Miss Havergal enjoyed delicate health, but wrote much poetry and other devotional material, composed music and threw herself so far as she could into religious and other good works. Among her best-known hymns is 'Take my life, and let it be'.
Hensley, Lewis (1824–1905) Anglican clergyman, held various appointments, including canon of St Albans.
Herbert, George (1593–1633) Came from noble family, favourite of King James I. Then became Rector of Bemerton in

Wiltshire. Distinguished poet, keen musician. May well have sung his own poems and hymns.

Hodgetts, Michael (1936–) Roman Catholic layman, actively involved in the work of the International Commission on English in the Liturgy. Has written a number of psalm paraphrases, new translations of ancient hymns and other worship material. Some appears in the *New Catholic Hymnal*.

Hopkins, John (d. 1570?) Collaborator with Thomas Sternhold (*q.v.*) in early, widely used metrical psalter (pub. 1562).

How, William Walsham (1823–97) Held various Anglican appointments, finally Bishop of Wakefield. Hymn-writer and editor of hymn-books. Wrote 'For all the saints' and 'It is a thing most wonderful'.

Idle, Christopher Martin (1938–) Held various Anglican appointments, currently Curate in Charge, St Matthias', Poplar, London. Contributor to *Psalm Praise*.

Jones, Richard (1926–) Methodist minister, currently serving with the Northern Baptist College, Manchester.

Kaan, Frederik (Fred) Herman (1929–) United Reformed Church minister. Has served with the World Council of Churches; now Moderator of U.R.C. West Midlands Province. Prolific hymn-writer; many of his hymns have achieved widespread acceptance.

Keble, John (1792–1866) Leader, with Newman and Pusey of the High Church Oxford Movement, but remained within the Church of England, becoming Vicar of Hursley, near Winchester. Professor of Poetry, Oxford in 1833. Prolific hymn-writer.

Ken, Thomas (1637–1711) Held various Anglican appointments, including Bishop of Bath and Wells. Took an uncompromising moral stand on a number of political issues.

Kethe, William (d. about 1600) Scottish (?). For a time, Protestant exile in Geneva. Early writer of metrical psalms.

Luther, Martin (1483–1546) Great Reformation leader. Realised the value of music and hymns in propagating the Reformed faith. A keen musician, wrote hymns and wrote or adapted tunes.

Lyte, Henry Francis (1793–1847) Native of Ireland, held various appointments in the Church of Ireland, afterwards Church of England, particularly the West Country. Wrote a number of psalm-based hymns.

Milton, John (1608–74) Great poet, author of *Paradise Lost.* Prominent supporter of Cromwell during the Civil War and Commonwealth.

Monsell, John Samuel Bewley (1811–75) Native of Ireland, held several Anglican appointments, finally Rector of St Nicholas, Guildford. Described as a 'persuasive preacher and a singularly devout and sunny-hearted man', he wrote eleven volumes of poetry, as well as hymns.

Montgomery, James (1771–1854) Son of an Ulster Scot who was a Moravian minister. Became editor of *The Sheffield Iris* newspaper for 31 years, but his liberal and radical political views created trouble. Enthusiastic supporter of foreign missions. Wrote 40 hymns, mostly early in his life. The first English hymnologist.

Neander, Joachim (1650–80) Distinguished German Reformed Church theologian, writer, poet, and musician. Suffered some persecution. Belonged to the Pietist movement. Wrote about 60 hymns.

Newman, John Henry (1801–90) As Vicar of St Mary the Virgin, Oxford, leader of the Oxford Movement with Pusey and Keble (*q.v.*). Became a Roman Catholic, finally being made a Cardinal. Considerable literary gifts and achievements.

Newton, John (1725–1807) After a wild life, including experience of the slave trade, was converted by George Whitfield, ordained in the Church of England, and became an influential leader of the Evangelicals and Abolitionists. Collaborated with his friend, William Cowper (*q.v.*) in writing *Olney Hymns,* himself contributing 280.

Noel, Caroline Maria (1817–77) Daughter of an Anglican clergyman. She suffered deteriorating health, and wrote her hymns to pass on to others the comfort she received from God.

Rous, Francis (1579–1659) M.P. and member of Cromwell's

Council of State. Wrote metrical psalms, which were collated with those of William Barton (*q.v.*) in the Scottish Psalter.

Ryland, John (1753–1825) Baptist minister, a founder and later Secretary of the Baptist Missionary Society. Wrote almost 100 hymns.

Sidney, Sir Philip (1554–86) and *Sidney, Mary, Countess of Pembroke* (1550?–1621) Brother and sister who collaborated on a metrical psalter. Sir Philip was a distinguished poet and man of letters. Famous as a courtier and one-time favourite of Queen Elizabeth I, for his character, charm and accomplishments.

Smith, Walter Chalmers (1824–1908) Held several appointments as minister in the Free Church of Scotland, including Moderator of the Assembly. Prolific religious poet and author.

Steele, Ann (1717–78) One of the first women in England to publish hymns. Her work was directly inspired by the appearance of a Baptist hymn-book in Bristol in 1769.

Sternhold, Thomas (d. 1549) Employed in the courts of Henry VIII and Edward VI. Wrote early metrical psalms and set them to music. His work was collated with that of John Hopkins (*q.v.*).

Tate, Nahum (1652–1715) Irishman of very limited poetical gifts who nevertheless became Poet Laureate. Wrote metrical psalms and other paraphrases with Nicholas Brady (*q.v.*).

Watts, Isaac (1674–1748) Refused a university education, rather than conform to the Church of England. Studied at a dissenting academy and remained an Independent. Spent six years as tutor to the children of Sir John Hartopp, then became minister of Mark Lane Independent Church, London. His health failed and he lived as an invalid guest of Sir Thomas Abney. Wrote poetry, text-book on logic, metrical paraphrases and hymns. Notable for his tolerance and liberal views. By the quality of his hymns, helped to establish hymn-singing in British Churches, and helped to improve relationships between Anglicans and Nonconformists.

Weissel, Georg (1590–1635) Important early Prussian hymn-writer, composing about 20 hymns. Minister of the Church at Königsberg.

Wesley, Charles (1707–88) Younger brother of John (*q.v.*) and one of the greatest of all hymn-writers, composing about 6,500. His hymns were instrumental in founding Methodism, and were greatly used by John. Charles himself strongly disapproved of a separate denomination outside the Church of England.

Wesley, John (1703–91) Founder of Methodism, and leading religious figure of the eighteenth century. Published many books, including grammars, dictionaries and translations of the classics, besides journals, sermons, etc. Translated some German hymns and was active in emending the hymns of others, not always for the better.

Winkworth, Catherine (1829–78) Very active and usually very good translator of German hymns, helped to make them available to the British Churches. Friend of distinguished literary and religious figures such as Charles Kingsley and Charlotte Brontë. Pioneer of women's education.

Wither, George (1588–1667) Prolific poet. He annoyed James I, served in Charles I's army in Scotland, changed sides to the Roundheads and was imprisoned at the Restoration. Wrote some hymns which may be undervalued, others which are eccentric, as for instance 'On the Presentation of Twins to the Organist' and 'On the Bursting of the Kitchen Boiler'.

Wordsworth, Christopher (1807–85) Nephew of the poet. Bishop of Lincoln. Hardworking pastor and author, writing many hymns which are sometimes over-didactic.

Index of Hymns

Index of Psalms